Acclaim for Kate Bornstein's

GENDER OUTLAW

"While Bornstein covers an incredible range—from the 'nuts and bolts' of her surgery to more abstract musings on a brave new gender-free world—the book never stops fascinating. [She offers us] an abundance of questions—thoughtful, disarming, revelatory questions. *Gender Outlaw* is an invitation to a dialogue, and it's a conversation well worth having." —*Ms.*

"Kate Bornstein argues eloquently and passionately for scrapping the categories of women and men. Agree. Disagree. Read it!"
—Leslie Feinberg, author of *Stone Butch Blues*

"The first book of gender theory written by a transgendered person . . . includes countless insights, trenchant cultural analysis, and generous wit. . . . [It] will surely become a classic."
—*Washington Blade*

"[Bornstein is on the] leading edge of contemporary debate about sexual identity and gender. [She] asks fundamental and challenging questions about what it means to be a man or woman in our society." —*San Francisco Chronicle*

"Kate is an orgasm on two legs. Reading this book gives me a heart orgasm, and it could give you one too! *Gender Outlaw* is a great work of love." —Annie Sprinkle, performance artist

"Kate Bornstein is a fierce and funny voice on the front lines of gender and sexual identity. Her wise heart and wild imagination challenge us to really own our bodies, our desires, our dreams."

—Tim Miller, performance artist

Kate Bornstein

GENDER OUTLAW

Kate Bornstein divides their time between New York City and the Rhode Island shore. She can be seen in all episodes of season two of the reality TV show *I Am Cait*. Their stage work includes the solo performance pieces *The Opposite Sex Is Neither*, *Virtually Yours*, and *On Men, Women, and the Rest of Us*. When not writing or performing, Kate can be found cuddling with Maui, following *Doctor Who*, prowling Twitter and Instagram, or playing pinball in their hometown of Asbury Park, New Jersey.

GENDER OUTLAW

On Men, Women, and the Rest of Us

REVISED AND UPDATED

KATE BORNSTEIN

VINTAGE BOOKS

A Division of Penguin Random House LLC

New York

SECOND VINTAGE BOOKS EDITION, NOVEMBER 2016

Revised edition and introduction copyright © 2016 by Kate Bornstein

All rights reserved. Published in the United States by Vintage Books, a division of Penguin Random House LLC, New York, and distributed in Canada by Random House of Canada, a division of Penguin Random House Canada Limited, Toronto. Originally published in hardcover in the United States by Routledge, New York, and simultaneously in Great Britain by Routledge, London, in 1994. Copyright © 1994 by Routledge. Subsequently published in paperback, with a new afterword, by Vintage Books, a division of Penguin Random House LLC, New York, in 1995.

Vintage and colophon are registered trademarks of Penguin Random House LLC.

The author gratefully acknowledges the permission of *Issues Monthly* (February 1991) to reprint "Nuts and Bolts" and "The Lesbian Thing" in this volume.

Photo credits: pg. iv, Sam Feder; pg. 278: Dona Ann McAdams; pg. 144: Glenn Tonneson; pg. 182: Ingrid White; pp. 186, 212: Jill Posener; pg. 210: David Harrison; pg. 276: Janet Van Ham.

The Cataloging-in-Publication data is on file at the Library of Congress.

Vintage Books Trade Paperback ISBN: 978-1-101-97324-0
eBook ISBN: 978-1-101-97461-2

www.vintagebooks.com

Printed in the United States of America

10   9   8   7

This book is dedicated to my friend and teacher, John Emigh,
who taught me about laughter and acting,
who showed me it was okay to break some rules and to follow some others,
who responded to my gender change with both respect
and a good sense of humor,
and who encouraged me to continue working in theater
when I was sure I'd have to give it up.
Bless you and thank you, John—
you've always asked me challenging questions.

———————————

In Loving Memory of:

Doris Fish
'Tippi'
Lou Sullivan
Tedde Matthews
John Payne
Leland Moss
Ethyl Eichelberger
Charles Ludlam
Kelly
Christine Jorgensen
and
Billy Tipton

come see what's on the inside!

Gender Is a Wooly Worm   xi

Part One First Things First

1   Transgender Style: Some Fashion Tips   5

Part Two Sorting Seeds

2   The Hard Part   9

3   Interlude: Nuts and Bolts   19

4   Naming All the Parts   25

5   Interlude: The Lesbian Thing   51

6   Abandon Your Tedious Search: The Rule Book Has Been Found!   55

Part Three Claiming Power

7   Which Outlaws?: or, Who Was That Masked Man?   67

8   Gender Terror, Gender Rage   91

9   Send in the Clowns   111

10   First You Die, and Then You Get Their Attention   121

Part Four A Gender Interrogatory

11   The First Question: or, They Have Those Funny, Staring Eyes   131

12   The Other Questions   145

Part Five **Creating a Third Space**

13   Transsexual Lesbian Playwright Tells All!   183

14   Queer Life / Queer Theater   187

Part Six **Hidden: A Gender**

15   *Hidden: A Gender*: a play in two acts   213

Part Seven **The Punchline**

16   The Seven Year Itch: (What Goes Around, Comes Around)   279

Acknowledgments   293

Bibliography   297

GENDER IS A WOOLY WORM

Welcome to the almost-silver-anniversary
edition of *Gender Outlaw*

When you translate the playful title **Gender Outlaw** into Mandarin, it comes out as the not-so-playful **Sex Criminal**. So my Chinese publisher, New Star Press, asked me for some other titles. I rummaged through my mind for familiar gender metaphors and hopped onto Skype with my translator, Liao Aiwan, who uses the pronouns **they**, **them**, and **theirs**.

"How about **Gender Is a Butterfly**?" I suggested.

"No, no," they said. "This book of yours is a radical call to gender activism. To a Chinese reader, **butterfly** makes it seem like a fluffy children's book. But the butterfly metaphor is certainly in the right ballpark."

I suggested **Gender Is a Cocoon**, and they explained to me that to a Chinese mind, the image of a cocoon conjures the panic that comes with claustrophobia. We both stared at each other blankly. Then their face lit up.

"Gender Is a Caterpillar! It's perfect!"

"Ah," was all I could think to say.

Liao Aiwan explained that, to a Chinese reader, the caterpillar stage conjures the notion of great possibilities. "That's what you're trying to say about gender, isn't it? Possibilities?"

I nodded; yep, that's what I was going for with the book. They continued excitedly, saying that we should use the child's term **wooly worm** because that gets us back to playful. And so, if you want to buy this book in China, look for the title **Gender Is a Wooly Worm**.

"Just like you wanted **gender outlaw** to be playful. Right, Kate?"

Just so. And between the two of us, we found a common language of gender.

So . . . what's **your** language of gender?

With whom do you talk about gender?

Are there people who speak a language of gender that doesn't quite make sense to you?

The language of gender that I learned growing up in the fifties was all in service to the difference between men and women. White men and white women, to be specific. And the earliest differences were biology. In the early 1980s, I knew for a fact that I could never be a woman so long as I had a penis. So I transitioned from male to female by means of gender confirmation surgery—it was the only way I could possibly live as the woman I believed myself to be. In Denmark some fifty years earlier, Lili Elbe knew for a fact that she could never be a woman so long as she had no uterus. Miss Elbe died from complications resulting from *her* gender confirmation surgery, an attempted uterus transplant. At that time, the trans story began with hormones and ended with surgery. But stories shift over time and culture, as does the language used to tell them.

There's not just one trans story. There's not just one trans experience. And I think what they need to understand is that not everybody who is born feels that their gender identity is in alignment with what they're assigned at birth, based on their genitalia. If someone needs to express their gender in a way that is different, that is okay, and they should not be denied healthcare. They should not be bullied. They don't deserve to be victims of violence. . . . That's what people need to understand, that it's okay and that if you are uncomfortable with it, then you need to look at yourself.

—*Laverne Cox (**Time** magazine,*
May 29, 2014)

Recently I had the great pleasure of introducing Ms. Cox and her twin brother, M Lamar, at a speaking gig they were doing in New York City. Backstage, they thanked me—told me that they'd read **Gender Outlaw** in college and that it had been a great help. I thanked them in return, saying that the two of them had taken the exploration and expression of gender much further than I'd ever dreamed while I was first writing this book.

The study of gender parallels the study of particle physics, in that both fields have made, um, quantum leaps over the past fifty or sixty years. I grew up understanding subatomics as protons, neutrons, and electrons—that was the sum total of public discourse on the subject. As more and more sophisticated methods of investigation were developed, more and more basic particles were discovered—and the language of physics expanded in response to more and more in-depth study of quantum particles. I was sixteen years old when the quark model was first proposed. In the same way that our understanding of particle physics has grown more nuanced, we today speak casually about many finely honed nuances of gender that never occurred to me when I first sat down to write this book.

The point now, in these early days [of particle physics], is to investigate physical systems of a sort that just haven't existed before.

—Jeff Kimble

My experience of gender—the whole big deal about why I got to write this book—was that I experienced myself as not-man, not-woman. And not too many of us were talking about that in the first person. Not-man, not-woman—I defined myself by what I was not. Today, tens of thousands of people who understand themselves to be not-men, not-women use words that describe *precisely* who they are: femme-identified nonbinary trans, or gender nonconforming, or agender, or transmasculine genderqueer, and so forth. The permutations of identity and expression are seemingly endless. I've done my best to take all that into account when I wrote this updated edition.

Happily, the basic concepts I was writing about then still hold true—but I needed to tweak the words I used to describe those basic concepts. For example, in the original we used the word *transgendered*. Yep—it never occurred to us that the suffix *-ed* implied that transgender was something that had been done to us. Live and learn. Furthermore, the word *transgender* was an inclusive term for anyone who was messing with gender. To this day, a great many people still use *transgender* like that: an umbrella term for anyone for whom the management of gender consumes a great deal of their day-to-day attention. But in the broader discourse, out in mass media, *transgender* has shifted meanings. Today, *trans* is the term that's inclusive of people's myriad experiences of gender. *Transgender* today simply means a man or a woman who has transitioned from another gender. That's what we used to call *transsexual*—and to be fair, there are many people who still today understand their transition to be a physical journey that brings their bodies into alignment with their gender identities. But by and large, today's transgender men and women understand that it's not sex-as-biology that's essential to life, but rather gender-as-identity. So, I've gone through the book with as fine-toothed a comb as I could to make changes to bring that up to date.

> And of course, language will continue to change. In five, ten, fifty years, the language used to describe gender will become even more nuanced. More identities and expressions of gender will emerge, necessitating ever more changing definitions.

Additionally, our narrow view of gender back then was radically different from today's intersectional perspective. Today, we know that gender is impacted by at least a dozen inescapable modifiers: class, race, age, disability, mental health, religion, family and children, politics, looks, language, and habitat and ecology. Back when I was writing this book, we isolated gender from its many entanglements. Well, physicists study particles by isolating atoms and photons in huge particle colliders, just to see what actually happens when one lone particle is hit by another. While we've learned the importance of context, the study of gender in the absence of all its cultural modifiers can still give us a clear picture of the mechanics of gender phenomena. My second book, *My Gender Workbook*, and its recent new edition, *My New Gender Workbook*, do embrace a more intersectional analysis, and thereby a more nuanced view of gender as it plays itself out in day-to-day living.

In the first edition of this book, the word *binary* wasn't being used at all. Instead, I variously used *two-gender* and *bi-polar* gender. But *binary* and *nonbinary* are a good deal more helpful to understanding and parsing gender today—so I think it's important I define *binary* as I understand it.

Imagine, please, a circle. Anything and everything about gender is inside that circle. Now, divide that circle with a vertical line so that you've got two equal parts. Anything and everything about gender is still inside the circle, only now it's got to fit on one side or another—and everything on one side has an opposite counterpart on the other side. Got it? For any aspect of gender to grow beyond its designated place on one side, it's got to encroach upon the space of the other side. In this way, every bit of growth on one side is seen as an attack on the other side. This is a binary system of culture—in form, a binary system is a battlefield.

Now, if you introduce an element into that binary system that clearly does not belong on one side or the other, you shatter the binary into innumerable components. You've still got a circle, and that circle still includes anything and everything about gender. Only now, there are lots of binaries: man and woman, girl and boy, butch and femme, lady and gentleman, and so on. And there are spectrums of gender in that circle. Any way you can imagine looking at gender can exist peacefully alongside every other way of looking at gender. The circle is no longer a binary—it's a dialectic. In form, a dialectic system is a playground.

A quarter century ago, the idea of transitioning from one gender to another was against the binary cultural law of gender that very clearly said Thou Shalt Not Transition. And so, transsexuals—those of us who saw ourselves as men and women in need of a physical transition—were gender outlaws. Today, trans men and trans women routinely tell me that they are not gender outlaws. And I agree. The idea of gender transitions from M to F and F to M has reached a tipping point, and so today's transgender men and women live well in accordance with the binary view of gender: they are not gender outlaws. If anything, they are gender *in-laws*, along with people who identify as cisgender (people whose gender identity corresponds to the biological sex they were assigned at birth).

It's wonderful to see such a proliferation of nonbinary gender identities and expressions these days. When this book first came out, the idea of an identity other than one of two genders was literally unthinkable—we couldn't wrap our minds around it. Not so much now. Now, nonbinary genders are deliciously problematic in the LGBTQ paradigm of sexuality and gender that we're currently working with. In LGBTQ, nonbinary gender identities currently can occupy either the T or the Q. On the other hand, nonbinary genders can also be seen as the third that shatters the binary of cisgender and transgender. Deliciously problematic.

I understand today that for many people, cis and trans alike, it's a good deal more comforting to work with gender as a binary—but the either/or of it was never a comfort to me. All I knew to express, all those years ago, was in today's language:

BINARY GENDER = BAD
NONBINARY GENDER = GOOD

Of course that's not true. It's a binary notion that's been targeted by critics of my ideas of gender. In this edition, I've done my best to break that binary with a more nuanced analysis.

Now, this brings me to one more point of this book that needs some clarification. Many people have taken exception to my idea that gender needs to be done away with entirely. Well, it's been almost twenty-five years, and I've come to see that a little more clearly: we need to do away with any system of gender that pressures us into believing that we are imperfectly gendered. The gender I'm perfectly happy with keeping around is the gender I live with that shifts on its own accord as I move forward in time and space. After all, our genders are one of many ways that we interface with others, and with our surroundings. I believe that if we simply trust ourselves to shift, sure enough, our genders will shift as we need them to. Chameleons don't decide to change colors. I'm totally fine with that kind of gender. The rest of it? The gender that mandates a right way or wrong way? Yeah, that needs to be done away with.

I'm grateful to Vintage Books for giving me a do-over. I'm especially thankful to my editors, Catherine Tung and Emily Giglierano. Publishing, like theater, is much more of a cooperative effort—my editors are excellent dramaturges and a lot of fun to work with.

They also agreed with me that it would be best to keep some sections of the book exactly as they first appeared:

1. Those artistic expressions of neither/nor gender, as in the play *Hidden: A Gender*, or the performance pieces "Transsexual Lesbian Playwright Tells All!" and "The Seven Year Itch."
2. Those snapshots of a time when gender-as-biology was just beginning to come to a screeching halt (as in the sections covering transsexual surgery and queer theater).

Crafting this new edition came down to translating my language from a culture that existed in time and space a quarter of a century ago. And so I'd like to close *this* introduction by quoting a section of my introduction to the Chinese translation of this book, *Gender Is a Wooly Worm*:

> When I first wrote this book, language was a big problem. People knew about transsexuals. But not many people were talking about the phenomenon of people who are neither men nor women, no matter how they choose to express their gender. To embrace those people (myself included), I borrowed the word **transgender**. But in many circles today, that word has become simply another word for transsexual—so in my country, the newer and more inclusive word is simply **trans**. You will read words in this book that don't ring true to you. Please, take a pen or pencil and cross them out. Write in a word you like better. And when that word doesn't work for you anymore, use another word. The way of gender is a living, changing path, like a river—it does no one any good to try to keep either gender or a river still.
>
> The language you discover may be useful to others, so please share it with them. Write blogs, poetry, drama, and films that use **your** language for gender. Meet with other people who are finding **their** words, and discuss the value of language in the search for freedom and fluidity in gender. Your language may make others angry.

Their language may make you laugh. That's all part of the fun.

Now, if anything you read in this book makes you feel bad or wrong or small and weak, then please know that I said something wrong. This book was written many years ago, and the culture I wrote it in is not the culture in which you're reading it. So, if you find anything to be personally insulting, please accept my apology and keep reading with the knowledge that your gender identity and how you express your gender are correct only when you feel they are correct.

In closing, I'd like you to know that I'm writing this to you at the age of sixty-eight. I'm very old. I may very well be alive as you're reading these words. But if I'm dead, I would be honored if you call upon me as your ancestor in our mutual journey of gender exploration. I promise you that alive or dead, I will do all that's in my power to help you find and live your destiny.

Much Love and Respect,
Kate Bornstein

GENDER
OUTLAW

LIFE WITH FATHER
AND MOTHER
BEGAN FOR

ALBERT
HERMAN

MARCH
15ᵀᴴ

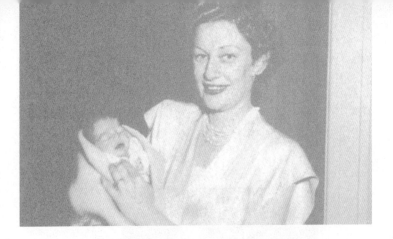

first things first

I keep trying to integrate my life. I keep trying to make all the pieces into one piece. As a result, my identity becomes my body, which becomes my fashion, which becomes my writing style. Then I perform what I've written in an effort to integrate my life, and that becomes my identity, after a fashion.

My mother was so proud to have given birth to a son. Our love and friendship grew into much more than either mother-son or mother-daughter.

|

TRANSGENDER STYLE

Some Fashion Tips

> People are starting to ask me about fashion. I love that! Maybe they think the doctor sewed in some fashion sense during my genital conversion surgery.

I see fashion as a proclamation or manifestation of identity—so as long as identities are important, fashion will continue to be important. The link between fashion and identity begins to get real interesting, however, in the case of people who don't fall clearly into a culturally recognized identity—people like me. My identity as a transsexual lesbian whose female lesbian lover transitioned to gay male is manifest in my fashion statement—both my identity and fashion are based on collage. You know—a little bit from here, a little bit from there? Sort of a cut-and-paste thing.

> And that's the style of this book. It's a trans style, I suppose. I can see it in the work of Susan Stryker, Sandy Stone, David Harrison . . . the list is getting longer and longer.

But the need for a recognizable identity, and the need to belong to a group of people with a similar identity—these are driving forces in our culture, and nowhere is this more evident than in the areas of gender and sexuality. Hence the clear division between fashion statements of male and female, between the fashions of queer and straight.

In my case, however, it's not so clear. I identify as neither male nor female, and now that my lover went through his gender change, it turns out I'm neither hetero nor homo. What I've found as a result of this borderline life is that the more fluid my identity has become—and the less demanding my own need to belong to the camps of male, female, gay, or straight—the more playful and less regimented my fashion has become—as well as my overall style of self-expression.

> **Will the identification with a trans writing style produce an identification with a trans experience?**

Anyone who knows fashion will tell you that the operative word is *accessorize*! That's how I dress in the morning. That's how I shift from one phase of my life to the next—first I try on the accessories. And that's also part of the style of this book: I've added some accessories here and there to spice it up a bit.

Welcome to my runway!

sorting seeds

The very first task that Psyche had to accomplish in her search to be reunited with her lover, Eros, was to sort, by type, a roomful of seeds. According to the myth, these seeds covered the floor and rose to nearly the height of the ceiling. I spent the first thirty years of my life sorting out the cultural seeds of gender and sexuality.

In the backyard of our house on the Jersey Shore. I'm about two years old.

2

THE HARD PART

The novel being dead, there is no point to writing made-up stories. Look at the French who will not and the Americans who cannot. Look at me who ought not, if only because I exist entirely outside the usual human experience . . . outside and yet wholly relevant, for I am the New Woman whose astonishing history is a poignant amalgam of vulgar dreams and knife-sharp realities (shall I ever be free of the dull lingering pain that is my peculiar glory, the price so joyously paid for being Myra Breckinridge, whom no man may possess except on her . . . my terms!).

—Gore Vidal, Myra Breckinridge, 1968

The hard part was sorting it all out. The hard part was taking a good look at everyone else and the way they looked at the world, which was a lot different from the way I was looking at the world!

There are some trans people who agree with the way I look at the world, and there are others who are really angry with me for writing this stuff. Every trans person I know went through a gender transformation for different reasons, and there are as many truthful experiences of gender as there are people who think they have a gender.

I know I'm not a man—about that much I'm very clear, and I've come to the conclusion that I'm probably not a woman either, at least not according to a lot of people's rules on this sort of thing. The trouble is, we're living in a world that insists we be one or the other—a world that doesn't bother to tell us exactly what one or the other *is*.

When I was a kid, everyone else seemed to know they were boys or girls or men or women. That's something I've never known; not then, not today. I never got to say to the grown-ups, "Hold on there—just what is it about me that makes you think I'm a little boy?" As a kid, I just figured I was the crazy one; I was the one who had some serious defect.

For most of my life, my nontraditional gender identity has been my biggest secret, my deepest shame. It's not that I didn't want to talk about this with someone; it's just that I never saw anything in the culture that encouraged me to talk about my feeling that I was a different gender than most people believed me to be. When I was growing up, people who lived cross-gender lives were pressured into hiding deep within the darkest closets they could find. Those who came out of their closets were either studied under a microscope, ridiculed in the tabloids, or made exotic in pornography, so it paid to hide. It paid to lie. That was probably the most painful part of it: the lying to friends and family and lovers, the pretending to be someone I wasn't. Going through a gender change is not the easiest thing in the world to do, but I went through it because I was so tired of all the lies and secrets.

> It was a strange kind of lie. It was a lie by action—I was always acting out something that everyone assumed I was. I wonder what it would have been like if someone had come along and in a quite friendly manner had asked, "Well, young one, what do you think you are: a boy or a girl— or something else entirely?" What would it have been like not to have been afraid of getting hit because of some wrong answer? See, what we used to call "sex changes" never were an appropriate topic of conversation—not at the dining table, not in the locker room, not over a casual lunch in a crowded restaurant.

Nowadays, I try to make it easier for people to ask questions. I tell people that I've never been hurt by an honest question, and that's true—it's a cruel opinion that hurts, never a question. But people still don't ask questions easily; maybe that has something to do with manners or etiquette. Despite the increased visibility of trans people, folks seem to naturally back off from inquiring as to the nature of someone's—my—gender. It seems to need some special setting. Like in my living room, or on television, or from behind a podium at some university. It's "good manners" to say and ask nothing, and that's sad. But the children still ask.

> Two days after my lover and I appeared on TV as guests on **The Phil Donahue Show**, the five-year-old child of our next-door neighbor came up to me and asked, "So, are

you a boy or a girl?" We'd been living next door to these folks for over two years.

"I'm a girl who used to be a boy," I replied. She was delighted with that answer and told me I'd looked very pretty on television. I thanked her and we smiled at each other and went about our days. I love it that kids will just ask.

Adults don't ask. Adults are afraid to ask, "What are you?" so we ask, "What do you do?" or "What's your pronoun of choice?" . . . in hopes of getting a clue to someone's identity. Gender identity seems to be an unspeakable thing in our culture, just as names are considered unspeakable in some other cultures. By the same token, we hardly ever ask outright, "What kind of sex do you like?" When it comes to work, we can ask. When it comes to sex and gender, we're supposed to observe discreetly and draw our own conclusions.

Instead of asking directly, adults look in roundabout ways for answers to their questions about me and my people. Like reading transsexual and transvestite pornography, which, judging by much of its content, must be written by people who have never met one of us but who must have great longing to be or love who we are.

There's this entire wonderful underground genre of trans erotica. You may have seen some of the titles—they're terrific—like **He's Her Sister!** Or **Transvestite Marriage** or **Transvestite Trap**. My personal favorites were **Captive in Lace** and **They Made Him Love It!**

Reading those stories came in handy when I was doing phone sex for a living, because a lot of the men calling in wanted to be cross-dressed as women, or they wanted to know what it would be like to be a woman and have sex with another woman—guys want to know that sort of thing. They want to know, "What do lesbians do with each other?" It's a sad question, really: it shows how little thought they give to exactly what pleases a woman.

> There's another whole group of people who really **like** gender ambiguity; it turns them on. I remember a group of sailors in the audience on **The Geraldo Rivera Show**. After it was announced who and what I was, they kept on looking at me, they kept on wanting something. I could feel their eyes traveling up and down my surgically constructed, hormonally enhanced woman's body. What's the pull? What is it about a sexually blended, gender-bended body that lights those flames? I know it gets me going!

For the most part, people cautiously observe and don't ask questions, and there are plenty of opportunities in today's world to look at people like me. The talk show ratings go way up during sweeps month when they trot out the transgender folks, the cross-dressers, and those who claim nonbinary or genderqueer identities. There are the drag shows and the female-impersonator spectacles—even though we began them for our own entertainment and enjoyment, their widespread popularity seems to grow and grow; you've probably got one of those shows in your city, or in a nearby town. Or please, watch *RuPaul's Drag Race*. Right now. What's more, trans identities are a comedy staple—we're always good for a cheap laugh. I'll have more to say about that later.

Both popular music and cinema reflect my not-man, not-woman face back to me. Glance discreetly, if you will, at some of the brightest deities in our cultural heavens. At this writing, Miley

Cyrus has been out as nonbinary for several years, drawing cheers and jeers from around the world. Both *Orange Is the New Black* and *Transparent* have opened up story lines that include trans people who identify as neither men nor women. Nouveau cabaret artists are emerging onstage, with genders far too fabulous to be pinned down to man-or-woman.

> It's interesting that we can ask questions about trans issues when there's some distance between us and the person we're asking about—whether that distance is online, onstage, or onscreen; we just don't ask directly.

I read, watch, and listen to all the ads and commercials. You can learn a lot about gender from commercials. I've also been watching the talk shows, listening to the call-in programs, and browsing the myriad blogs and videos. When I was very young, growing up in the '50s, I read the medical texts, devoured the tabloids, and hoarded the pornography—because I was intensely interested in me and my people.

> I was scared, though, shaking scared, to see what I might actually find out. But I couldn't stop reading. See, I was a lonely, frightened little fat kid who felt there was something deeply wrong with me because I didn't feel like I was the gender I'd been assigned. I felt there was something wrong with me, something sick and twisted inside me, something very, very bad about me. And everything I read backed that up.

The possibility missed by most of the texts prior to the past few years, and by virtually all the various popular media, is this: the culture may not simply be creating roles for naturally gendered people, the culture may in fact be *creating* the gendered people. In other words, the culture may be creating gender. No one had ever hinted at that, and so, standing outside a "natural" gender, I thought I was some monster, and that it was all my fault.

In living along the borders of the gender frontier, I've come to see the gender system created by this culture as a particularly malevolent and divisive construct, made all the more dangerous by the seeming inability of the culture to *question* gender, its own creation. The studies conducted by the duly appointed representatives of the culture are still conducted less on the basis of conversation and more on observation. I want this book to begin to reverse that trend. I want this book to be the conversation I always wanted as I was growing up, and never had the chance to have.

The time for discreet and distant observation of trans lives seems to be coming to an end. There's more and more evidence that trans folks are making a place for themselves in the culture. I wrote this book, for example, and it got published because there's been a shift—that this is a new edition of this book says the shift is still going on some two decades later. Up until the turn of the century, all we'd be able to write *and get published* were our autobiographies, tales of women trapped in the bodies of men or men pining away in the bodies of women. Stories by and about brave nonbinary-identified people who'd lived their lives hiding deep within a false gender—and who, after much soul-searching, decided to change their gender, and spent the rest of their days hiding deep within *another* false gender. That's what we could get published about our nonbinary selves—the romantic stuff that set in stone our image as long-suffering, not the challenging stuff. And it always seemed that the people who would write *about* us either had some ax to grind or point to prove, or they'd been hurt and needed someone to blame it on. People like Janice Raymond, Catherine Millot, and Robert Stoller have ultimately perpetuated the myth that trans people are malevolent, mentally ill, or monsters. We got left holding the cultural bag. We ended up wearing the cultural hand-me-downs.

But there's another kind of trans(gressive)gender experience going on in this culture, and nowadays we're writing our own chronicles of these times. Our stories all tie together, our stories overlap; and you can hear lots about me in the stories of other trans people. My story weaves through Caitlyn Jenner's story. My story lies within the story of the late historian Louis Sullivan. Christine Jorgensen and Renée Richards wrote chapters of my story in their autobiographies. For years, Sandy Stone taught her story, my story, our story in any number of her classes. Rachel Pollack has painted trans into her tarot cards. Laura Jane Grace belts it out in punk rock and whispers it in her poetry. Gwen Smith makes archives available online. For decades, Leslie Feinberg traveled back and forth across the country to make our story heard in the political arena. Del LaGrace Volcano captures us in exquisite photographs. Lana and Lilly Wachowski bring us into their films. Mx. Justin Vivian Bond, Taylor Mac, Silvia Calderoni, David Harrison, and dozens more trans folk perform our story live onstage. Janet Mock, Laverne Cox, RuPaul, and dozens more trans people of color are bringing the intersections of gender, race, class, and age into mainstream media. Trans people are talking to one another at conferences around the world, in online meeting rooms, and through an increasing number of blogs, newsletters, and journals. It's an exciting time, here in the still-early days of a movement. It's a time when we've begun to put down the cultural baggage. We've begun sewing sequins onto our cultural hand-me-downs.

My voice on this subject is not representative of all trans people. But when a minority group has been silent for as long as we have, as disjointed as we have been, the tendency is for those in the majority to listen to the loud ones when they first speak up; and to believe that we speak for the entire group. More important than my point of view, than any single point of view, however, is that people begin to question gender.

For the past quarter of a century, the voices of trans people have been rising in concert with the voices of more and more people who are writing their work based on what we have to say. Suzanne Kessler, Wendy McKenna, Marjorie Garber, Jennie Livingston, Judith Butler, Wendy Chapkis, Anne Bolin, Walter Williams, and Shannon Bell are some of the earliest cisgender writers who have been asking great questions and making room for us to respond.

I've taken as much care as I can to encourage questions in this book, especially questions about my conclusions. I hope that soon after this book is published I'll have some more questions. Questions are the hard part.

3

INTERLUDE

Nuts and Bolts

To this day, most people in the world believe that gender is determined by one's genitals. It's no surprise that many transgender people have adopted that belief, pursuing genital conversion surgery in their quest for a full and complete transition. The following text is an interview I did on the subject with *Issues Magazine,* back in the early 1990s—when most trans people opted to prioritize surgical genital modification as a prerequisite to transition. Way back then, it was all about the ladies. Transgender men were only just beginning to emerge into cultural awareness.

On the Surgical Process

Issues: *All right. We'd like to start with the biological/technical questions, the "nuts and bolts," as it were . . .*

Kate: [laughing] . . . I bolted from mine, that's for sure . . .

Issues: *. . . could you talk a little bit about the entire process of the surgery and how it's done?*

Kate: It's a long process. It requires a year to two years of therapy, and then another therapist has to validate your therapist's opinion, for you to be qualified to go to a surgeon
and say, "See, they think I'm a girl." During that time you
can start hormones.

Before surgery you need to do what's called a "Life
Test," which is living as another gender for at least a year,
sometimes two years.

Issues: *What does that mean?*

Kate: Day and night. Before any kind of genital reassignment
surgery. In other words, if you were going to do this,
you'd have to live as a man for a year to two years to see
if you could function socially, if you could make a living.
For example, in *Hidden: A Gender*, the character Justin
Bond plays [Herculine Barbin] couldn't function socially
or economically as a man. And so that would have been
discovered and they would have said, "Hey, look. Give it
up. Go back." And some people cannot get it together to
function one way or the other. So you live that test, and
then you go through with genital surgery. I know mostly
about male-to-female surgery. There are two female-to-
male techniques. Both are fine, except that sometimes
they're not cosmetically up to snuff, so to speak.

Issues: *I was going to ask whether women can become men, because a
lot more of the sex changes you hear about are men becoming
women.*

Kate: Ah, the qualifier is that you *hear* about it; it's about 50-50.

Issues: *Where does the penis come from?*

Kate: Well, in one technique they take a skin graft, either from
the inner thigh or the belly, literally roll it up, and attach
it at the top of the thigh and the bottom of the belly.
Then the patient has to lie in bed for four weeks or so
while this heals up, to make sure the blood is going fine.
So you've basically got what looks like a suitcase handle.

They then remove one end from the thigh, so the suitcase handle is hanging down from the bottom of the belly. They don't have a way to extend the urethra through this penis, so the man must pee through the same urethral opening he had when he was a woman. Some men keep their vaginas, some have their vaginas partially sewn up.

Issues: *Okay. So what about men to women?*

Kate: The most common technique is the one I had: it's called "penile inversion." They lay the penis out and make an incision down the length of it, pull the skin open, scrape out the spongy stuff, being very careful not to disturb the blood vessels and nerves. The scrotal sac is laid open, the testicles are removed and become compost, I guess [general laughter]. So then they take the tip of the penis and start pushing it in. Kind of like turning a sock inside out. Everyone has this natural cavity, right, so they just push it in . . .

Issues: *They invert it.*

Kate: Yah, exactly. So that the outside of the penis becomes the walls of the new vagina. The tip of the penis functions in the position of a cervix. They create a kind of clitoris, using the spongy material from the perineum. And then they hope for the best. The real tricky part of the surgery is the urethra. You're catheterized, because if you can't pee, you die. So that's real important. And they place this big pack in there while everything heals for about five days, and then they remove the pack and you have to keep dilating your new vagina by putting this little balloon thing in, and pumping it up, and letting it dilate for about twenty minutes, five or six times a day.

One of the comic things that you're told about before surgery, which is so frightening, but funny in retrospect, is that when the pack has been in there, it's pushed up against this new urethral opening, and the catheter's been pushing it, so the urethral opening is pushed over to the side, so you don't know in which direction you're going to pee when you finally pee. So when I sat down to pee, it shot straight up in the air, and I was like, "Oh noooooooooo!" But eventually it gets itself into the right position and you pee in the right direction.

There's a doctor at Stanford who performs this penile inversion technique who takes a section, about half an inch, of intestine, which is a mucous membrane, and also grafts that in there, so that it will lubricate, because it is, in fact, membranous tissue. I don't lubricate, so if I'm going to have any kind of penetration I need lubrication. The disadvantage to that technique is that it never stops lubricating, so you're kind of always wet and sloppy [smiles]. Which doesn't *have* to be a disadvantage.

Issues: *How much did all this cost?*

Kate: Remember, this was 1985–86: it was four thousand dollars for the nine days in the hospital, and four thousand dollars to the doctor. Then there was the round-trip airfare, it was in Colorado . . . there's lots of fees involved in this. Blue Cross ended up paying for it. It took a while to process because of a computer fuckup. They had put in "genital surgery" as a category, and they had my gender listed as female. Well, the only category that the computer could find vaguely near genital surgery was circumcision, and when it saw *circumcision* and *female,* it created a loop that it couldn't get out of. So it just spun around in the computer for a while.

On Hormones

Issues: *So this actual surgery happens after taking the hormones for a while? It's the last step?*

Kate: It's what they consider the final step, yah. And what happened with me was I got my surgery about seven months after I'd started taking hormones, because the hormones have different effects on people. Yes, they can cause breast growth, but this [referring to her chest] mostly grew after surgery. What happened with me is that my penis started shrinking incredibly while I was taking hormones. And the doctor said, "If I don't do the surgery now, we're going to have to add a skin graft from your butt or your thigh, so that you can have some kind of depth." I'd already told him that I didn't need much depth; [smiles] that wasn't what I was concerned with.

Issues: *What other effects did the hormones have?*

Kate: They changed the texture of my skin—my skin's a lot softer. They caused breast growth. I'm on a hormonal regimen now of what they would give most women after a hysterectomy, who still have a uterus. I take Premarin every day, which is estrogen, and then seven days a month I take progesterone.

Issues: *You're going to be taking that forever?*

Kate: Forever. Unless I want to go through menopause again. . . . I went through all the "classic symptoms" of menopause when I was getting onto hormones initially. While I was still producing my own testosterone, I had to take these massive doses of estrogen to overcome that. I'd sit at my desk at work and cry a lot. And now, I've got seven days a month of raging PMS. The only thing I don't ever do is have cramps or bleed. But I get the water retention, the mood swings, and all that.

On Orgasms

Issues: *What is actually stimulated during orgasm? And where is it?*

Kate: There are different kinds of orgasm. My vaginal walls are more sensitive than your vaginal walls, your clitoris is more sensitive than my clitoris. I can be stimulated to clitoral orgasm. That's a lot of fun. Actually much more so than with a vaginal orgasm. It's been changing. But I can have a vaginal orgasm just by the stimulation of the vaginal walls. That's kind of nifty, too. I do have a lack of sensation in my labia. I can feel pressure, but the surface of the skin does not have any sensation. So there was a certain amount of nerve damage there.

These days, not all transgender people opt for genital modification—and many decide against taking hormones. Nonetheless, surgical and hormonal body modifications are essential to many trans people. The desire to change our appearance or presentation has always been present in trans people—it's just a matter of method and degree. All such changes—or lack of changes—are worthy of our respect.

My Bar Mitzvah: March 4, 1961, "Today I am a man."

4

NAMING ALL THE PARTS

For the first thirty or so years of my life, I didn't listen, I didn't ask questions, I didn't talk, I didn't deal with gender—I avoided the dilemma as best I could. I lived frantically on the edge of my white male privilege, and it wasn't 'til I got into therapy around the issue of what was then called my transsexualism that I began to take apart gender and really examine it from several sides. As I looked at each facet of gender, I needed to fix it with a label or definition, just long enough for me to realize that each label and definition I came up with was entirely inadequate and needed to be abandoned in search of deeper meaning.

> Labels and definitions—and the language itself—have their uses in much the same way that road signs make it easy to travel: they point out the directions. But you don't get to where you're going when you just stand underneath some sign, waiting for it to tell you what to do.

I took the first steps of my journey by trying to define the phenomenon I was daily becoming.

> There's a real simple way to look at gender: once upon a time, someone drew a line

in the sands of a culture and proclaimed with great self-importance, "On this side, you are a man; on the other side, you are a woman." It's time for the winds of change to blow that line away. Simple.

Gender means *class*. By calling gender a system of classification, we can dismantle the system and examine its components. Suzanne Kessler and Wendy McKenna in their landmark 1978 book *Gender: An Ethnomethodological Approach* open the door to viewing gender as a social construct. They pinpoint various phenomena of gender, as follows:

Gender Assignment

Gender assignment happens when the culture says, "This is what you are." In most cultures, we're assigned a gender at birth—and once you've been assigned a gender, that's what you are and always will be. For the most part, it's doctors who dole out the gender assignments, which shows you how emphatically gender has been medicalized. These doctors look down at a newly born infant and say, "It has a penis, it's a boy." Or they say, "It doesn't have a penis, it's a girl." It has little or nothing to do with vulvas or vaginas, let alone DNA, hormones, or dozens of other nuances of biological sex. It's all penises or no penises: gender assignment is both phallocentric and genital. Other cultures are not or have not been so rigid.

In the early nineteenth century, Kodiak Islanders would occasionally assign a female gender to a child with a penis: this resulted in a woman who would bring great good luck to her husband, and a larger dowry to her parents. For many decades, the European umbrella term for this and any other type of first-nation trans person was *berdache*. Walter Williams in *The Spirit and the Flesh* chronicles nearly as many types of berdache as there were nations in the Americas.

Even as early as 1702, a French explorer who lived for four years among the Il-linois Indians noted that berdaches were known "from their childhood, when they are seen frequently picking up the spade, the spindle, the ax [women's tools], but making no use of the bow and arrow as all the other small boys do."

—Pierre Liette, "Memoir of Pierre Liette
on the Illinois Country"

When the gender of a child was in question in some Navajo tribes, they reached a decision by putting a child inside a tipi with a loom and a bow and arrow—female and male implements, respectively. They set fire to the tipi, and whatever the child grabbed as he/she ran out determined the child's gender. It was perfectly natural to these Navajo that the child had some say in determining its own gender. Compare this method with the following modern example:

[The Montana Educational Telecommu-nications Network, an early online bulle-tin board] enabled students in tiny rural schools to communicate with students around the world. Cynthia Denton, until last year a teacher at the only public school in Hobson, Montana (popula-tion 200), describes the benefit of such links. "When we got our first messages from Japan, a wonderful little fifth-grade girl named Michelle was asked if she was a boy or a girl. She was extraordi-narily indignant at that, and said, 'I'm Michelle—I'm a girl of course.' Then I pointed out the name of the person who

had asked the question and said, 'Do
you know if this is a boy or a girl?' She
said, 'No, how am I supposed to know
that?' I said, 'Oh, the rest of the world
is supposed to know that Michelle is a
girl, but you have no social responsibility
to know if this is a boy or a girl?' She
stopped and said, 'Oh.' And then she re-
phrased her reply considerably."

—Jacques Leslie, "The Cursor Cowboy," 1993

Is the determination of one another's gender a "social responsibility"?

Do we have the legal, moral, or ethical right
to decide and assign our own genders?

Or does that right belong to the state, the
church, and the medical profession?

If gender is classification, can we afford to
throw away the very basic right to classify ourselves?

Gender Identity

Gender identity answers the question, "Who am I?" Am I a man
or a woman or a what? It's a decision made by nearly every individual, and it's subject to any influence: peer pressure, advertising, drugs, cultural definitions of gender, whatever.

Gender identity is assumed by many to be "natural"—that
is, someone can feel "like a man," or "like a woman." When I
first started giving talks about gender, this was the one type of
question that would keep coming up: "Do you feel like a woman
now?" "Did you ever feel like a man?" "How did you know what
a woman would feel like?"

I've no idea what "a woman" feels like. I never did feel like a girl or a woman; rather, it was my unshakable conviction that I was not a boy or a man. It was the absence of a feeling, rather than its presence, that convinced me to change my gender.

> What **does** a man feel like?
> What does a woman feel like?
> Do **you** feel "like a man"?
> Do you feel "like a woman"?
> I'd really like to know that from people.

Gender identity answers another question: "To which gender (class) do I want to belong?" Being and belonging are closely related concepts when it comes to gender. I felt I was a woman (being), and more important I felt I belonged with other women (belonging). In this culture, the only two sanctioned gender clubs are "men" and "women." If you don't belong to one or the other, you're told in no uncertain terms to sign up fast.

> Sweet Loretta Martin
> Thought she was a woman
> But she was another man.
> All the girls around her
> Thought she had it coming
> But she gets it while she can.
> Get back, get back,
> Get back to where you once
>   belonged.
> Get back, Loretta.
>
> > —John Lennon and Paul McCartney,
> > "Get Back," 1969

> I remember a dream I had when I was no more than seven or eight years old—I might have been younger. In this dream, two

lines of battle were drawn up facing each other on a devastated plain: I remember the earth was dry and cracked. An army of men on one side faced an army of women on the other. The soldiers on both sides were exhausted. They were all wearing skins—I remember smelling the untanned leather in my dream. I was a young boy, on the side of the men, and I was being tied down to a roughly hewn cart. I wasn't struggling. When I was completely secured, the men attached a long rope to the cart and tossed the other end of the rope over to the women. The soldiers of the women's army slowly pulled me across the empty ground between the two armies, as the sun began to rise. I could see only the sun and the sky. When I'd been pulled over to the side of the women, they untied me, turned their backs to the men, and we all walked away. I looked back and saw the men walking away from us. We were all silent.

I wonder about reincarnation. I wonder how a child could have had a dream like that in such detail. I told this dream to the psychiatrist at the army induction center in Boston in 1969—they'd asked if I'd ever had any strange dreams, so I told them this one. They gave me a 1-Y, deferred duty due to psychiatric instability.

Gender Roles

Gender roles are collections of factors that answer the question, "How do I need to function so that society perceives me as belonging or not belonging to a specific gender?" Some people would include appearance, sexual orientation, and methods of communication under the term, but I think it makes more sense to also think in terms of things like jobs, economic roles, chores, hobbies; in other words, positions and actions specific to a given gender as defined by a culture. Gender roles, when followed, send signals of membership in a given gender.

Gender Expression

Gender expression is how we put our gender identity into play out in the world—and like gender identity, the manner in which we express our gender(s) is for us alone to decide. Components of gender expression include but are not limited to: clothing, body modification, speech, posture, movement, language, attitude—whatever it takes for us to experience integrity, fulfillment, and joy. Gender expression is how we garner a desired gender attribution from others.

Gender Attribution

Then there's gender attribution, whereby we look at somebody and say, "That's a man," or "That's a woman." And this is important because the way we perceive another's gender affects the way we relate to that person. Gender attribution is the sneaky one. It's the one we do all the time without thinking about it; kinda like driving an eighteen-wheeler down a crowded highway . . . without thinking about it.

In this culture, gender attribution, like gender assignment, is phallocentric. That is, one is assumed to be male until perceived otherwise. According to a study done by Kessler and McKenna, one can extrapolate that it would take the presence of roughly four female cues to outweigh the presence of one male cue. That's one reason why more trans women today get "sirred" whereas fewer trans men get called "ma'am."

Gender attribution depends on cues given by the attributee and cues perceived by the attributer. The categories of cues as I have looked at them apply to a man/woman binary gender system, although they could be relevant to a more fluidly gendered system. I found these cues to be useful in training actors in cross-gender role-playing: body, hair, clothes, voice, skin, and movement.

> I'm nearly six feet tall, and I'm large-boned. Like most people assigned male at birth, my hands, feet, and forearms are proportionally larger to my body as a whole than those of people assigned female at birth. My hair pattern included coarse facial hair. My voice is naturally deep—I sang bass in a high school choir and quartet. I've had to study ways and means of either changing these physical cues or drawing attention away from them if I want to achieve a female attribution from people. See, I know I'm not a woman, but as long as most people believe there are only two options for gender, my great joy is walking through the world **as a woman**.

Susan Brownmiller's book *Femininity* is an excellent analysis of the social impact of physical factors as gender cues.

Behavioral cues include manners, decorum, protocol, and deportment. Like physical cues, behavioral cues are relative to the contexts of time and culture. Most advice websites freely dispense gender-specific manners. The majority of the behavioral cues I can think of boils down to how we occupy space, both alone and with others.

Some points of manners are not taught in books of etiquette. Rather, they are signals we learn from one another, mostly signals acknowledging membership to an upper- (male-) or lower- (female-) gendered class. But to commit some of *these* manners in writing in terms of gender-specific behavior would be an acknowledgment that gender exists as a class system.

Here's one: As part of learning to pass as a woman, I was taught to avoid eye contact when walking down the street; that looking someone in the eye was a male cue. Nowadays, sometimes I'll look away, and sometimes I'll look someone in the eyes— it's a behavior pattern that's more fun to play with than to follow rigidly. A femme cue (not "woman," but "femme") is to meet someone's eyes (usually a butch), glance quickly away, then slowly look back into the butch's eyes and hold that gaze: great, hot fun, that one! None of this is written down or even particularly enforceable, but in my part of the world, all of this was required for membership in the gender **woman**. (Of interest is that these are also universal cues of submission.)

In many of the transsexual and transvestite support meetings I've attended, when the subject of the discussion was "passing," a lot of emphasis was given to manners: Who stands up to shake hands? Who exits an elevator first? Who opens doors? Who lights cigarettes? These are all cues I had to learn in order to pass as a woman in this culture. It wasn't 'til I began to read feminist literature that I began to question these cues or to see them as oppressive.

Textual cues include histories, documents, names, associates, relationships—true or false—that support a desired gender attribution. Someone trying to be taken for male in this culture might take the name Bernard, which would probably get a better male attribution than the name Brenda.

Changing my name from Al to Kate was no big deal in Pennsylvania. It was a simple matter of filing a form with the court and publishing the name change in some unobtrusive "notices" column of a court-approved newspaper. Bingo! Done. The problems came with changing all my documents. The driver's license was particularly interesting. Prior to my full transition, I'd been pulled over once already dressed as a woman, yet holding my male driver's license—it wasn't something I cared to repeat.

Any changes in licenses had to be done in person at the Department of Motor Vehicles. I was working in corporate America: Ford Aerospace. On my lunch break, I went down to the DMV and waited in line with the other folks who had changes to make to their licenses. The male officer at the desk was flirting with me, and I didn't know what to do with that, so I kept looking away. When I finally got to the desk, he asked, "Well, young lady, what can we do for you?"

"I've got to make a name change on my license," I mumbled.

"Just get married?" he asked jovially.

"Uh, no," I replied.

"Oh! Divorced!" he proclaimed with just a bit of hope in his voice. "Let's see your license." I handed him my old driver's license with my male name on it. He glanced down at the card, apparently not registering what he saw. "You just go on over there, honey, and take your test. We'll have you fixed up soon. Oh," he added with a wink, "if you need anything special, you just come back here and ask old Fred."

I left old Fred and joined the line for my test. I handed the next officer both my license and my court order authorizing my name change. This time, the officer didn't give my license a cursory glance. He kept looking at me, then down at the paper, then me, then the paper. His face grim, he pointed over to the direction of the testing booths. On my way over to the booths, old Fred called out, "Honey, they treating you all right?" Before I could reply, the second officer snarled at old Fred to "get your butt over" to look at all my paperwork.

I reached the testing booths and looked back just in time to see a quite crestfallen old Fred looking at me, then the paper, then me, then the paper.

Mythic cues include cultural and subcultural myths that support membership in a given gender. This culture's myths include archetypes like: weaker sex, dumb blonde, strong silent type, and better half. Various waves of the women's movement have had to deal with a multitude of myths of male superiority, and the freakishness that is nonbinary gender.

Power dynamics as cue include modes of communication, communication techniques, and degrees of aggressiveness, assertiveness, persistence, and ambition.

Sexual orientation as cue highlights, in the dominant culture, the heterosexual imperative (or in the lesbian and gay culture, the homosexual imperative). For this reason, many male heterosexual transvestites who wish to pass as female will go out on a "date" with another man (who is dressed as a man)—the two seem to be a heterosexual couple. In glancing at the "woman" of the two, an inner dialogue might go, "It's wearing a dress, and it's hanging on the arm of a man, so it must be a woman."

For the same man to pass as a female in a lesbian bar, he'd need to be with a woman, dressed as a woman, as a "date."

> I remember one Fourth of July evening in Philadelphia, about a year after my surgery. I was walking home arm in arm with Lisa, my lover at the time, after the fireworks display. We were leaning in to each other, walking like lovers walk. Coming toward us was a family of five: mom, dad, and three teenage boys. "Look, it's a coupla faggots," said one of the boys. "Nah, it's two girls," said another. "That's enough outta you," bellowed the father. "One of 'em's got to be a man. This is America!"

Sexuality and gender are discrete phenomena. Depending on the qualifier one is using for gender differentiation, sexuality and gender may or may not be seen as dependent on each other.

There are probably as many types of gender (gender systems) as could be imagined. Gender by clothing, gender by divine right, gender by lottery—these all make as much sense as any other criteria. But in Western civilization, we bow down to the great gods of medical science. And so, no other type of gender holds as much sway as:

Biological gender, as determined by science and documented by the state, which is the most universally respected gender cue—it most nearly always guarantees a desired attribution. Bio gender (or sex) classifies a person through any combination of body type, chromosomes, hormones, genitals, reproductive organs, or some other corporal or chemical essence. Belief in biological gender is in fact a belief in the supremacy of the body in the determination of identity. It's biological gender that most folks refer to when they say *sex*. By calling something "sex," we grant it seniority over all the other types of gender—by some right of biology.

So, all these *parts* of gender determine *types* of gender that in and of themselves are *not* gender, but criteria for systemic classification. And there's sex, which somehow winds up on top of the heap. Add to this roomful of seeds the words *male, female, masculine, feminine, man, woman, boy, girl*. These words fall under the category of gender and are highly subjective, depending on which system of gender one is following.

But none of this explains why there is such a widespread insistence upon the conflation of *sex* and *gender*. I think a larger question is why Eurocentric culture needs to see *so much* in terms of both sex (classification by biology) and sexuality (classification by whoopee).

It's not like gender is the **only** thing we confuse with sex. As a culture, we're encouraged to equate sex (both the act and the biology) with money, success, and security; and with the products we're told will help us attain money, success, and security. We live in a culture that succeeds in selling products (the apex of accomplishment in capitalism) by aligning those products with the attainment of one's sexual fantasies and gender identity.

Switching my gender knocked me for a time curiously out of the loop of ads designed for men or women, heteros or homos. I got to look at both biological sex and sexuality without the hype, and ads without the allure. None of them, after all, spoke to me, although all of them beckoned.

Kinds of Sex

"Can you orgasm with that vagina?"
   —Audience member question for Kate on The
                    Geraldo Rivera Show

It's important to keep gender and sex separated as, respectively, system and function. Since function is easier to pin down than system, sex is a simpler starting place than gender.

"Yah, the plumbing works and so does the electricity."
                    —Kate's answer

Sex does have a primary factor to it that is germane to a discussion of gender: sexual orientation, which is what people call it if they believe you're born with it, or sexual preference, which is what people call it if they believe you have more of a choice and more of a say in the matter.

The upshot is that sex (the biological act) is defined (culturally dependent upon) as sex (the biological identity). Please keep in mind that what we are calling sex (biological gender) is as ephemeral as any other gender, because determining sex/gender by the presence or absence of a penis is at best a haphazard guess as it negates all the other factors of biological identity. And that brings us giddily back to *what is sex?*

> [W]e do not need a sophisticated methodology or technology to confirm that the gender component of identity is the most important one articulated during sex. Nearly everyone (except for bisexuals, perhaps) regards it as the prime criterion for choosing a sex partner.
>
> —Murray S. Davis, Smut: Erotic Reality/
> Obscene Ideology, 1983

The Basic Mix-Up

> A gay man who lived in Khartoum
> Took a lesbian up to his room.
> They argued all night
> Over who had the right
> To do what, and with what, to whom.
>
> —Anonymous limerick

Here's the tangle that I found: sexual orientation/preference is based in this culture solely on the gender of one's partner of choice—thus we make sex, sexuality, and gender all tangled up by their dependence upon one another. And so, the only choices we're given to determine the focus of our sexual desire are these:

» *Heterosexual model*: in which a culturally defined male is in a relationship with a culturally defined female.

» *Gay male model*: two culturally defined men involved with each other.
» *Lesbian model*: two culturally defined women involved with each other.
» *Bisexual model*: culturally defined men and women who could be involved with either culturally defined men or women.

Variants to these gender-based relationship dynamics would include heterosexual female with gay male, gay male with lesbian woman, lesbian woman with heterosexual woman, gay male with bisexual male, and so forth. People involved in these variants know that each dynamic is different from the other. A lesbian involved with another lesbian, for example, is in a very different relationship than that of a lesbian involved with a bisexual woman, and *that's* distinct from being a lesbian woman involved with a heterosexual woman. What these variants have in common is that each of these combinations forms its own clearly recognizable dynamic, acknowledged or not by the dominant cultural binary of sexual orientation: heterosexuality / homosexuality.

> And if we are going to use gender as a condition or basis of sexuality, we are sooner or later obliged to include trans as a factor of desire. Just now there is no agreed-upon word for the desire and desirability of trans bodies. The TV show **Transparent** came up with **transamorous**. Now doesn't that just blow apart the binary of homo-or-hetero?

So, all current mainstream-approved models of sexuality depend on the gender of the partner. This results in minimizing, if not completely dismissing, other dynamic models of desire and relationship that could be more important than gender and are often more telling about the real nature of someone's sexual desire. In the same way that there are many ways beyond simple biology to parse gender identity and gender expression, there are many factors on which we *could* base sexual orientation. Examples of alternate dynamic models include:

» *Butch/Femme model*, however that may be defined by its participants.

Butch style, whether worn by men or women, is a symbol of detachment. Dressing butch gives the wearer the protection of being the observer, not the object. A femme-y look, by contrast, suggests self-display, whether in a quietly demure or sexually flashy fashion. Butch is a style of understatement: "I don't need to show flesh because I am in a position to choose." Butch is no coy "come hither" look, but a challenge—"I see you and maybe I like what I see."

There is something about femme-y style that in itself produces insecurity, a sense of vulnerability and exposure. The femme invites the gaze and it takes a great deal of feminine self-confidence to risk that kind of scrutiny.

—Wendy Chapkis, Beauty Secrets: Women and the Politics of Appearance, 1986

» *Top/Bottom model*, which can be further subclassified as dominant/submissive or sadist/masochist.

The bottom is responsible for being obedient, for carrying out her top's or-

*ders with dispatch and grace, for being
as aroused and sexually available and
desirable as possible, and for letting her
top know when she is physically uncomfortable or needs a break. . . . The top
is responsible for constructing a scene
that falls within the bottom's limits, although it is permissible to stretch her
limit if she suddenly discovers the ca-
pacity to go further than she ever has
before.*

—*Patrick Califia,* Sapphistry: The Book of
Lesbian Sexuality, *1983*

There are also:

> *Butch/Butch models*
> *Femme/Femme models*
> *Triad (or more) models*
> *Human/Animal models*
> *Adult/Child models*
> *Same-aged models*
> *Parent/Child models*
> *Multiple partners models*
> *Able-bodied models*
> *Differently-abled bodies models*
> *Reproductive models*
> *Owner/Slave models*
> *Monogamous models*
> *Polyamorous models*

I'm sure I'm leaving models out of this, and someone is going
to be really upset that I didn't think of them; but the point is
there's more to sex (both the act and the biological identity) than
gender (one classification of identity).

Try making a list of ways in which sexual preference or orientation could be measured in your own life, and then add to that list (or subtract from it) every day for a month, or a year (or for the rest of your life). Could be fun!

Sex Without Gender

There are plenty of instances in which sexual attraction can have absolutely nothing to do with the gender of one's partner.

When Batman and Catwoman try to get it on sexually, it only works when they are both in their caped crusader outfits. Naked heterosexuality is a miserable failure between them. . . . When they encounter each other in costume however something much sexier happens and the only thing missing is a really good scene where we get to hear the delicious sound of Catwoman's latex rubbing on Batman's black rubber/leather skin. To me their flirtation in capes looked queer precisely because it was not heterosexual, they were not man and woman, they were bat and cat, or latex and rubber, or feminist and vigilante: gender became irrelevant and sexuality was dependent on many other factors. . . .

You could also read their sexual encounters as the kind of sex play between gay men and lesbians that we

*are hearing so much about recently:
in other words, the sexual encounter is
queer because both partners are queer
and the genders of the participants are
less relevant. Just because Batman is
male and Catwoman is female does not
make their interactions heterosexual—
think about it, there is nothing straight
about two people getting it on in rubber
and latex costumes, wearing eyemasks
and carrying whips and other accoutre-
ments.*

—*Judith Halberstam, "Queer Creatures," On
Our Backs, Nov/Dec 1992*

Sexual preference *could* be based on genital preference. (This is not the same as saying preference for a specific gender, unless you're basing your definition of gender on the presence or absence of some combination of genitals.) Preference could also be based on the kind of sex *acts* one prefers, and, in fact, elaborate systems exist to distinguish just that, and to announce it to the world at large. For example, here's a handkerchief code from the Samois Collective's *Coming to Power*. The code is used for displaying preference in sexual behavior. Colors mean active if worn on the left side, or passive if worn on the right.

Left Side	Color	Right Side
Fist Fucker	Red	Fist fuckee
Anal Sex, Top	Dark Blue	Anal Sex, Bottom
Oral Sex, Top	Light Blue	Oral Sex, Bottom
Light S/M, Top	Robin's-Egg Blue	Light S/M, Bottom
Foot Fetish, Top	Mustard	Foot Fetish, Bottom
Anything Goes, Top	Orange	Anything Goes, Bottom
Gives Golden Showers	Yellow	Wants Golden Showers

Left Side	Color	Right Side
Hustler, Selling	Green	Hustler, Buying
Uniforms/Military, Top	Olive Drab	Uniforms/Military, Bottom
Likes Novices, Chickenhawk	White	Novice (or Virgin)
Victorian Scenes, Top	White Lace	Victorian Scenes, Bottom
Does Bondage	Gray	Wants to Be Put in Bondage
Shit Scenes, Top	Brown	Shit Scenes, Bottom
Heavy S/M & Whipping, Top	Black	Heavy S/M & Whipping, Bottom
Piercer	Purple	Piercee
Likes Menstruating Women	Maroon	Is Menstruating
Group Sex, Top	Lavender	Group Sex, Bottom
Breast Fondler	Pink	Breast Fondlee

I love this code! It gave me quite a few ideas when I first read it. But despite the many variations possible, sexual orientation/ preference remains culturally linked to our gender system (and by extension to our gender identity, biological or otherwise) through the fact that it's most usually based on the gender of one's partner.

The conflation of sex, sexuality, and gender affects more than individuals and relationships—it contributes to the linking together of the very distinct subcultures of gays, lesbians, bisexuals, leather sexers, sex workers, and trans people.

> A common misconception is that male cross-dressers are both gay and prostitutes, whereas the truth of the matter is that most cross-dressers that I've met hold down more mainstream jobs, careers, or professions, are married, and are practicing heterosexuals.

A dominant culture tends to combine its subcultures into manageable units. As a result, those who practice nontraditional sex are seen by members of the dominant culture (as well as by members of sex and gender subcultures) as a whole with those who embody nontraditional gender roles and identities. Any work to deconstruct the gender system needs to take into account the artificial amalgam of subcultures, which might itself collapse if the confusion of terms holding it together were to be settled.

In any case, if we buy into categories of sexual orientation based solely on gender—heterosexual, homosexual, bisexual, and even transamorous—we're cheating ourselves of a searching examination of our real sexual preferences. In the same fashion, by subscribing to the categories of gender based solely on some presumed male/female binary, we cheat ourselves of a searching examination of our real gender identity.

Trans and Desirability

I was not an unattractive man. People's reactions to my gender transition often included the remonstrative, "But you're such a good-looking guy!" Nowadays, as I navigate the waters between male and female, there are still people attracted to me, precisely because of the blend of genders I physically present. At first, my reaction was fear: "What kind of pervert," I thought, "would be attracted to a freak like me?" As I got over that internalized phobia of my transgender status, I began to get curious about the nexus of desire, sex, and identity. When, for example, I talk about the need to do away with gender, I always get looks of horror from the audience: "What about desire and attraction?" they want to know. "How can you have desire with no gender?" They've got a good point: the concepts of sexuality and gender seem to overlap around the phenomenon of desire. So I began to explore my trans identity's relationship to desire.

About five months into living full-time as a woman, I woke up one morning and felt really good about the day. I got dressed for work, and checking the mirror before I left, I liked what I saw—at last! I opened the door to leave the building, only to find two workmen standing on the porch, the hand of one poised to knock on the door. This workman's face lit up when he saw me. "Well!" he said. "Don't you look beautiful today." At that moment, I realized I didn't know how to respond to that. I felt like a deer caught in the headlights of an oncoming truck. I really wasn't prepared for people to be attracted to me. It took me a long time to comfortably respond to a man who's attracted to me—I never mastered the rituals of male/female attraction.

To me, desire is a wish to experience someone or something that I've never experienced, or that I'm not currently experiencing. Usually, I need an identity appropriate (or appropriately inappropriate) to the context in which I want to experience that person or thing. This context could be anything: a romantic involvement, a tennis match, or a boat trip up a canal. On a boat trip up the canal, I could appropriately be a passenger or a crew member. In a tennis match, I could be a player, an audience member, a concessionaire, a referee, a member of the grounds staff. In the context of a romantic involvement, it gets less obvious about what I need to be in order to have an appropriate identity, but I would need to have *some* identity. Given that most romantic or sexual involvements in this culture are defined by the genders of the partners, the *most* appropriate identity to have in a romantic relationship would be a gender identity, or something that passes for gender identity, like a gender role. A gender role could be, for example, any role that signifies butch, femme, top, or bottom—these are all methods of acting. So, even without one of two approved gender identities per se, some workable identity can be called up and put into motion within a relationship.

> When we play with our identities, we play with desire. Some identities stimulate desire, others diminish desire. To make ourselves attractive to someone, we modify our identity, or at least the appearance of an identity—and this includes gender identity.

I love being without an identity—it gives me a lot of room to play around—but it makes me dizzy, having nowhere to hang my hat. When I get too tired of not having an identity, I take one on: it doesn't really matter what identity I take on, as long as it's recognizable. I can be a writer, a lover, a confidante, a femme, a top, or a woman. I retreat into definition as a way of demarcating my space, a way of saying, "Step back, I'm getting crowded here." By saying, "I am the [fill in the blank]," I also say, "You are not, and so you are not in my space." Thus, I achieve privacy. Gender identity is a form of self-definition: something into which we can withdraw, from which we can glean a degree of privacy from time to time, and with which we can, to a limited degree, manipulate desire.

Our culture is obsessed with desire: it drives our economy. We come right out and say we're going to stimulate desire for goods and services, and so we're bombarded daily with ads and commercial announcements geared to make us desire things. No wonder the emphasis on desire spills over into the rest of our lives. No wonder I get panicked reactions from audiences when I suggest we eliminate gender as a system; gender defines our desire, and we don't know what we have if we don't have a gendered desire. Perhaps the more importance a culture places on desire, the more conflated become the concepts of sex, sexuality, and gender.

As an exercise, can you recall the last time you saw someone whose gender was ambiguous? Was this person attractive to you? And if you knew they called themselves neither a man nor a woman, what would it make you if you're attracted to that person? And if you were to kiss? Make love? What would you be?

> I remember one time at a gay and lesbian writers' conference in San Francisco, I was on a panel and asking these same questions. Because it was a specifically gay and lesbian audience, an audience that defined itself by its sexual orientation, I wanted to tweak them on that identity. I asked, "And what if I strapped on a dildo and made love to you: what would that make me?" Without missing a beat, panelist Carol Queen piped up, "Nostalgic."

5

INTERLUDE

The Lesbian Thing

Issues: *The thing that really fascinates me is that as a man, you were heterosexual, in the eyes of the construct, anyway. Did you feel like you were a man who was a lesbian?*

Kate: I didn't feel like I was a man. Ever. I was *being* a man, but I never felt like I was. I was, in every aspect, fulfilling the gender role of "man." The societal role of man. And so socially, I was a man. No question. But I never *felt* like I was.

Justin: *What is the difference between the way that heterosexual women related to you and the way that lesbians relate to you now?*

Kate: Real good question! When I was being a man relating with a woman, there was much more of an assumed "man role" and an assumed "woman role," and it was dichotomized. For the most part, there were certain constructs that were assumed, patterns of relating that are uniquely heterosexual that would be silly to try now. Now there's much more negotiating, much more talking, and much more fluidity in terms of roles in relating with women. Also, there's a distance in a heterosexual relationship. There can be a certain kind of getting together, but then there's always, "What the fuck *are* you anyway?"

It stops, it just stops. And in a lesbian relationship—and I'm assuming it's the same in a homosexual male relationship, I don't know—there's much more familiarity. There's just much more closeness.

Issues: *Were you ever attracted to men?*

Kate: I had fantasies about men. But was I ever attracted to a man? One [looks at Justin—they smile]. That was a crush, and I just couldn't understand it. "What is this?!" I was just hopelessly crushed out on Justin. And it was so intriguing. I've gotten over that to the point where I just love him so dearly, I just feel really close to him. But beyond that, no. I was never attracted to a man. I've had sex with men, prior to my surgery, and certainly not afterwards, and did not enjoy it. I still have fantasies, though, and they're fun, and sometimes during sex, my girlfriend and I would take turns strapping on dildos—which isn't the same as being a man or playing at being a man—and I'd look down at this thing and say, "Oh, I remember *that!*" [lots of laughter all around]. My lover says I'm more practiced than any of her other women lovers. It's lots of fun [laughter].

Acceptance in the Lesbian Community

Taste of Latex: *What's the reaction in the lesbian community to your being a transsexual lesbian? Were you seeking acceptance, and did you find it?*

Kate: I sought acceptance in one lesbian community that had a bad experience with a transsexual lesbian five or six years prior to my being there. According to women who were there, she had attempted a power play to take over this huge lesbian organization in the city, and the reaction was very strong, very vocal. The reaction was very much, "Well that's a man for you!"

Then I came along, and they were like, "LOOK OUT, another one!" People wouldn't know I was a transsexual and then they'd find out and they'd be like, "Oh, I knew all along: it was male energy, I felt that!" It was not very good acceptance. I [did find] acceptance with people much younger than me. People in their twenties and thirties were much more accepting than my generation, who are major fuddy-duds.

Now, it doesn't matter that much. I don't hang where I'm not accepted. I still get some people who have problems, who say, "Well, you're not really a woman," and I say, "Right . . ." And they say, "Well, how can you be a lesbian?" and to me that's the heart of it—I try to engage those folks by asking, "What's a woman? What's a man?" I wish someone would answer me that—it would make my life a lot easier. I could get on playing some other kind of game. But no one has been able to answer that. There's no hard and fast rule.

But there are rules. And there is a rule book.

Asbury Park Public School photo, about ten years old.

6

ABANDON YOUR TEDIOUS SEARCH

The Rule Book Has Been Found!

In the '80s, there were a lot of theories about addiction and codependence. Most of these agreed on the point that we get addicted to something in order to avoid or deny some other thing. Workaholics work, alcoholics drink, and sexaholics fuck. I look at unconscious gender in the same light: it's something we do to avoid or deny our full self-expression. People, I believe, compulsively act out gender—there actually are rules on how to do this.

I'd better not go too far on this, or someone will start a twelve-step program around this idea! Nonetheless, there **are** rules of gender.

The rules of gender are termed the "natural attitude" of our culture (the real, objective facts) per Harold Garfinkel's 1967 *Studies in Ethnomethodology*. I like to read these rules every now and then to see how each rule has continued to play a part in my life—it's frighteningly accurate. I keep in touch with these rules—it helps me figure out new ways of breaking them. Here are Mr. Garfinkel's rules, and a few ideas about each:*

1. There are two, and only two, genders (female and male).

The first question we usually ask new parents is: "Is it a boy or a girl?" There's a great answer to that one going around: "We don't know; they haven't told us yet." Personally, I think no question containing *either/or* deserves a serious answer, and that includes the question of gender.

> Back at the dawn of cyberspace, I used to hang out in chat rooms on a service called **America Online**. My screen name was **OutlawGal**. I inevitably got two queries: "What makes you an outlaw?" to which I'd always reply that I break the laws of nature. The second question was almost always "M or F?" to which I'd answer, "Yes." Anyone who had a sense of humor about that was someone I wanted to keep talking with.

2. One's gender is invariant. (If you are female/male, you always were female/male and you always will be female/male.)

The latest transsexual notable has been Renée Richards, who has succeeded in hitting the benefits of sex discrimination back into the male half of the court. The public recognition and success that

---

* Garfinkel, Harold. *Studies in Ethnomethodology*. Englewood Cliffs, NJ: Prentice-Hall, 1967.

it took Billie Jean King and women's
tennis years to get, Renée Richards has
achieved in one set. The new bumper
stickers might well read: "It takes cas-
trated balls to play women's tennis."

—Janice G. Raymond,
The Transsexual Empire, 1979

Despite her vicious attack on transsexuals, Raymond's book is a worthwhile read, chiefly for its intelligent highlighting of the male-dominated medical profession, and that profession's control of trans therapy, hormones, and surgery. Raymond and her followers believe in some essential thing called "woman," and some other essential thing called "man," and she sees trans women as encroaching on her space. Raymond obeys the rules: in her worldview, there can be no mutable gender.

> There have been both trans-excluding radical feminists and hard-line fundamentalists who have agreed that I was not only born male, but that no matter what happened to me, and no matter my choices, I will remain male 'til the day I die. I no longer dispute people like that: that's how they're going to experience me no matter what I say or do. As long as they neither threaten me nor keep me from entering any public space, I feel more sorry for them than anything else.

3. Genitals are the essential sign of gender. (A female is a person with a vagina; a male is a person with a penis.)

> I never hated my penis; I hated that it made me a man—in my own eyes, and in the

eyes of others. For my comfort, I needed a vagina—I was convinced that the only way I could live out what I thought to be my true gender was to have genital surgery to construct a vagina from my penis. Fortunately, I don't regret having done this.

It's real interesting all the papers you have to sign before actually getting male-to-female gender reassignment surgery. I had to acknowledge the possibility of every surgical mishap: from never having any sensation in my genitals, to never having another orgasm in my life, to the threat of my newly constructed labia falling off. As it turned out, I have some slight loss of feeling on the surface of the skin around my vagina, but I can achieve orgasm, and the last time I looked my labia were still in place. Like I said, I'm lucky; some folks aren't.

4. Any exceptions to two genders are not to be taken seriously. (They must be jokes, pathology, etc.)

I remember one time walking into a Woolworth's in Philadelphia. I'd been living as a woman for about a month. I came through the revolving doors and stood face-to-face with a security guard—a young man, maybe nineteen or twenty years old. He did a double take when he saw me and he began to laugh—very loud. He just laughed and laughed. I continued round through the revolving doors and left the store. I agreed with him that I was a joke; that I was the sick one.

> I went back in there almost a year later.
> Same guy was still there . . . and he came
> on to me.

5. There are no transfers from one gender to another
    except ceremonial ones (masquerades).

> The Mummers Parade is held annually on
> New Year's Day in Philadelphia. Hundreds
> of men—mostly blue-collar family men—
> dress up in sequins, feathers, and gowns,
> and parade up and down the main streets
> of the City of Brotherly Love.

In most shamanic cultures, there exists a ceremonial rite whereby
spiritual leaders, like the Siberian "soft man," need to live part of
their lives as another gender before attaining the rank of spiritual
leader.

*The transformation [from man to "soft
man"] takes place gradually when the
boy is between ages eight and fifteen,
the critical years when shamanistic inspiration usually manifests itself. The
Chukshi feel that this transformation is
due to powerful spirits.*
—Walter L. Williams, The Spirit and the Flesh,
1986

6. Everyone must be classified as a member of one
    gender or another. (There are no cases where gender is
    not attributed.)

Do you know anyone to whom you've not attributed the gender male or the gender female? Isn't that a hoot? That alone makes it important for each of us to question gender's grip on our society.

7. The male/female dichotomy is a "natural" one. (Males and females exist independently of scientists' [or anyone else's] criteria for being male or female.)

There is black on one side of a spectrum, and

white
on the other
with a middle ground of gray, or
some would say there's a rainbow between the two.

There is
left, and

right
and a middle ground of center.
There is birth on one side,

and death on the other side
and a middle ground of life.
Yet we insist that there are two,   And we insist that this
only two genders: male and female.   is the way of nature.

Blue

yellow
green.

Nature?

Nature?

Nature.

8. Membership in one gender or another is "natural." (Being female or male is not dependent on anyone's deciding what you are.)

In the mid-'80s, when I first got involved with women's politics, and gay and lesbian politics, I saw these buttons that read:

KEEP YOUR LAWS OFF MY BODY!

or

BIOLOGY IS NOT DESTINY!

I thought they were particularly relevant to my situation as a trans person. But I found out otherwise. If I attempt to decide my own gender, I am apparently transgressing against nature—never mind what the buttons said.

When I entered the women's community in the mid-'80s, I was told that I still had male energy. (I never knew what "male energy" was, but I later figured out that it was the last of my male privilege showing.) They said that I'd been socialized as a male and could never truly be a female; that what

I was, in fact, was a castrated male. And that hurt me for a long time—over a year, in fact.

I kept hearing people define me in terms *they* were comfortable with. It's easy to play victim, and to say that these people were being malicious, but assuming the worst about others is simply not truth, and it's not a loving or empowering way to look at other people. So, I began to look at their investment in defining me. What I found was that each person who was anxious to define me had a stake in maintaining his or her own membership in a given gender. I began to respect the needs of those who had a stake in their genders.

So I began to say things like, "Yep, I'm a castrated man all right, if that's what you see." And my joy at the look on their faces was the beginning of my sense of humor about all this—I was no longer humiliated by their definitions of me. I still have my Keep Your Laws Off My Body button:

In this day and age of bathroom legislation, it's more appropriate than ever.

Somewhere, Beyond the Rules

So there are rules to gender, but rules can be broken. On to the next secret of gender: gender can have ambiguity. There are many ways to transgress a prescribed gender code, depending upon the worldview of the person who's doing the transgressing: they range from preferring to be somewhat less than rigidly gendered, to preferring an entirely non-definable image. Achievement of these goals ranges from doing nothing, to maintaining several wardrobes, to full surgical transformation.

> It doesn't really matter what a person decides to do, or how radically a person plays with gender. What matters, I think, is how aware a person is of the options. How sad for a person to be missing out on some expression of identity, just for not knowing there are options.

And then I found out that gender can have fluidity, which is subtly different from ambiguity. If ambiguity is a refusal to fall within a prescribed gender code, then fluidity is the refusal to remain one gender or another. Gender fluidity is the ability to freely and knowingly become one or many of a limitless number of genders, for any length of time, at any rate of change. Gender fluidity recognizes no borders or rules of gender.

> A fluid identity, incidentally, is one way to solve problems with boundaries. As a person's identity keeps shifting, so do individual borders and boundaries. It's hard to cross a boundary that keeps moving!

It was the discovery of my own ambiguity and fluidity of gender that led me to my gender change. It was figuring out these two concepts that allowed me to observe these factors—inhibited or in full bloom—in the culture, and in individuals.

*At home in New Jersey, age thirteen or fourteen. I'd already
learned to smile for a camera, no matter what was going on.*

claiming power

I learned from working in the women's movement that one of the first steps in claiming power is to speak one's own voice: to name oneself. Having sorted out the culture's ideas of gender and sexuality, it's time to name the experience of stepping outside those ideas.

Launcelot Gobbo, the clown in Shakespeare's The Merchant of Venice, *at Faunce House Theater, Brown University, 1966, directed by Janice Van De Water Brown.*

7

WHICH OUTLAWS?

or, Who Was That Masked Man?

On the day of my birth, my grandparents gave me a television set. In 1948, this was a new and wonderful thing. It had a nine-inch screen embedded in a cherrywood case the size of my mother's large oven.

My parents gave over an entire room to the television set. It was "the television room."

I've tried to figure out which questions get to the core of transgender issues. The answer to the riddle of my oddly gendered life would probably be found in the many areas of gender we do not question. We talk casually, for example, about transgender without ever clearly stating, and rarely if ever asking, what one gender or the other really is. We're so sure of our ability to categorize people as either men or women that we neglect to ask ourselves some very basic questions: what is a man? and what is a woman? and why do we need to be one or the other?

If we ask by what criteria a person might classify someone as being either male or female, the answers appear to

be so self-evident as to make the ques-
tion trivial. But consider a list of items
that differentiate females from males.
There are none that always and without
exception are true of only one gender.

—*Kessler and McKenna,* Gender: An
Ethnomethodological Approach, *1970*

Touching All the Bases

Most folks would define a man by the presence of a penis or some form of a penis. Some would define a woman by the presence of a vagina or some form of a vagina. It's not that simple, though. I know several women in San Francisco who have penises. Many wonderful men in my life have vaginas. And there are quite a few people whose genitals fall somewhere between penises and vaginas. What are *they*?

Are you a man because you have an *XY* chromosome? A woman because you have *XX*? Unless you're an athlete who's been challenged in the area of gender representation, you probably haven't had a chromosome test to determine your gender. If you haven't had that test, then how do you know what bio sex you are? What gender you are? And how do you know the gender or even bio sex of your romantic and sexual partner(s)? There are, in addition to the *XX* and *XY* pairs, some other commonly occurring sets of gender chromosomes, including *XXY, XXX, YYX, XYY,* and *XO*. Does this mean there are more than two genders?

Let's keep looking. What makes a man—testosterone? What makes a woman—estrogen? If so, you could buy your gender over the counter at any pharmacy. But we're taught that there are these things called "male" and "female" hormones, and that testosterone dominates the gender hormone balance in the males of any species. Not really—female hyenas, for example, have naturally more testosterone than the males; the female clitoris resembles a very long penis—the females mount the males from the rear and proceed to hump. While some female humans I know behave in much the same manner as the female hyena, the example demonstrates that the universal key to gender is not hormones.

Are you a woman because you can bear children? Because you bleed every month? Many women are born without this potential, and every woman ceases to possess that capability after menopause—do these women cease being women? Does a necessary hysterectomy equal a gender change?

Are you a man because you can father children? What if your sperm count is too low? What if you were exposed to nuclear radiation and were rendered sterile? Are you then a woman?

Are you a woman because your birth certificate says female? A man because your birth certificate says male? If so, how did *that* happen? A doctor looked down at your crotch at birth. A doctor decided, based on what was showing of your external genitals, that you would be one bio sex (and thereby one gender) or another. You never had a say in that most irreversible of all pronouncements—and according to most cultures as they stand today, you never *will* have a say. What if you had been born with some combination of both genitals? A surgeon would have "fixed" you—without your consent, and possibly without the consent or even knowledge of your parents, depending on your race and economic status. You would have been fixed—fixed into a gender. Being born with different or anomalous genitals is more common than you might think, but we don't allow hermaphrodites in modern Western medicine. We "fix" them.

But let's get back to that birth certificate. Are you female or male because of what the law says? Is law immutable? Aren't we legislating every day in order to change the laws of our state, our nation, our culture? Isn't that the name of the game when it comes to political progress? What about other laws—religious laws, for example? Religions may dictate right and proper behavior for men and women, but no religion actually lays out what is a man and what is a woman. They assume we know, that's how deep this cultural assumption runs.

I've been searching all my life for a rock-bottom definition of woman, an unquestionable sense of what is a man. I've found nothing except the fickle definitions of gender held up by groups and individuals for their own purposes.

> Every day I watched it, that television told me what was a man and what was a woman.
>
> And every day I watched it, that television told me what to buy in order to be a woman. And everything I bought, I said to myself I am a real woman, and I never once admitted that I was trans. You could say I'm one inevitability of a postmodern anti-spiritualist acquisitive culture.
>
> But television is a primitive medium compared to the ever-evolving internet. And the internet is teaching more than either/ or gender, race, and age every day. That's a huge change from when I was growing up.

A Question of Priorities

I haven't found any answers to gender. I ask every day of my life what is a man and what is a woman, and those questions beg the next: why? Why do we have to be one or the other? Why do we have to be gendered creatures at all? What keeps the binary gender system in place?

I started out thinking that a theory of gender would bridge the long-standing gap between the two major genders, male and female. I'm no longer trying to do that. Some people think I want a world without gender, something bland and colorless: that's so far from how I live! I love playing with genders, and I love watching other people play with all the shades and flavors that gender can come in. I just want to question what we've been holding on to unconsciously for such an awfully long time. I want to question the reasoning behind the existence of gender, and I want to enter that questioning firmly into the fabric of this culture.

> I used to watch **The Lone Ranger** on television. I loved that show. This masked guy rides into town on a white horse, does all these great and heroic deeds, everyone falls in love with him, and then he leaves. He never takes off his mask, no one ever sees his face. He leaves behind a silver bullet and the memory of someone who can do no wrong. No bad rumors, no feet of clay, no cellulite. What a life! There's a self-help book in there somewhere. **Who Was That Masked Man?: Learning to Overcome the Lone Ranger Syndrome**.

As I moved through the 1950s and '60s, I bought into the fear and hatred that marks this culture's attitude toward gender nonconforming and agender people. Most folks are genuinely afraid of being without a gender. I've been chewing on that fear nearly all my life like it was some old bone, and now I want to take that fear apart to see what makes it tick. Nothing in the culture has encouraged me to stay and confront that fear. Instead, the culture has kept pointing me toward one door or the other:

Girls or Boys
Men or Women
Ladies or Gentlemen
Cats or Chicks

Faggots or Dykes
Drag Queens or Trans Women

I knew from age four on that something was wrong with me being a guy, and I spent most of my life avoiding the issue of my transsexuality. I hid out in textbooks, pulp fiction, and drugs and alcohol. I numbed my mind with everything from peyote to Scientology. I buried my head in the sands of television, college, a lot of lovers, and three marriages. Because I was being raised as a male, I never got to experience what it meant to be raised female in this culture. All I had were my observations, and all I could observe and assimilate as a child were differences in clothing, attitude, and manners. I remember building a catalogue of gestures, phrases, body language, and outfits in my head. I would practice all of these at night when my parents had gone to sleep. I'd wear a blanket as a dress, and I'd stand in front of my mirror being my latest crush at school. And because the culture I grew up in said that my childhood fantasies were perversions, I was so ashamed of myself.

> I was obsessed, and like most obsessed people, I was the last one to know it. The culture itself is obsessed with gender—and true to form, the culture as a whole will be the last to find out how obsessed it really has been.

Why We Haven't Asked Questions

I know there must have been other kids living as boys and girls, yet going through the same remorse-filled hell that held me prisoner in front of my bedroom mirror, we had no way of knowing that. There was no internet, no language for what we were doing. Instead, cardboard-cutout versions of us were creeping into the arts and media: in poetry, drama, dance, music, sculpture, paint-ing, television, cinema—in just about any art form you can think of there have been portrayals of people who are ambiguously or differently gendered, all drawn by people who were not us, all spoken in voices that were not ours. Thank goodness, that's changing. Thank goodness for the internet, where we've got a chance of learning about and connecting with one another.

> Dominant cultures attempt to colo-nize and control their margins through stereotyping—it's no different with the trans margins. In many areas of the world, it's still safe for someone to make a joke of us because there's no risk of our anger, no fear we'll raise some unified voice in protest, because we're not organized. But it's changing. It's more and more difficult to receive support for being mean to binary-identified trans people—people known in the media as transgender.

It's still pretty easy to get away with being mean to those of us who are agender, nonbinary, and gender nonconforming. We never did fit into the cultural binary of male/female, man/woman, boy/girl. No, we are the clowns, the sex objects, or the mysteriously unattainable in any number of novels. We are the psychotics, the murderers, or the criminal geniuses who popu-late the movies. Audiences are becoming more familiar with the reality of trans men and trans women—but audiences have rarely seen the real faces of the nonbinary, genderqueer, agender, and gender nonconforming. Our voices have gone unheard, our words have gone unread. For too many years, trans people of all stripes—binary and nonbinary alike—have been playing a hiding game, appearing in town one day, wearing a mask, and leaving when discovery was imminent. We would never tell anyone who we were, and so we were never really able to find one another. That's just now beginning to change.

> There are still too many places in the world where, when we walk into a restaurant and we see another trans person, we look the other way, we pretend we don't exist. There's never been a sly smile, no secret wink, signal, or handshake. In too many cultures and subcultures, we trans people still quake in solitude at the prospect of recognition, even if that solitude is in the company of our own kind.

Silence=Death

—ACT UP *slogan*

Silence of the Meek-as-Lambs

Simply saying "Come out, come out, wherever you are" is not going to bring the multitudes of trans people out into the open. Before saying that coming out is an option (and I believe it's an inevitable step, one we're all going to have to take at some time), it's necessary to get trans people talking with one another. The first step in coming out in the world is to set aside our different notions of gender, and come out and talk to our own kind.

> Transgender people (those who identify as men or women) and nonbinary trans people have been finding it difficult to get along with one another. It's another unconsciously supported binary we need to

> dissolve: binary gendered people and non-binary gendered people. We need to come to the understanding that each of us holds on to the truth of gender that most eases our suffering.

Before I transitioned, I had gold-card membership in the dominant culture. To all appearances, I was a straight, white, able-bodied, middle-class male. I fought so hard against being transsexual because I heard all the teasing and jokes in the locker rooms. I saw people shudder or giggle when they'd talk about Renée Richards or Christine Jorgensen. I was all too aware of the disgust people were going through when *Playboy* published its interview with Wendy Carlos. I watched Caroline Cossey (Tula) get dragged through the mud of the press on two continents. The lesson was there time after time. Of course we were silent.

> In the summer of 1969, I drove across Canada and the United States, living out of my Volkswagen station wagon, which I'd named Mad John after my acting teacher. I was a hippie boy, hair down past my shoulders and dressed very colorfully: beads, headband, bell-bottoms. I pulled into a state park in South Dakota to camp for the night. Some good ol' boys came up to my campsite and began the usual "Hey, girl" comments. I ignored them, and they eventually went away. Later that night, I woke up in my sleeping bag with a hand on my chest and a knife in front of my face. "Maybe we wanna fuck you, girl," is what this guy said. He brought the knife down to my face—I could feel how cold and sharp it was.

"Maybe you oughta get outta here before we fuck you and beat the shit outta you." Then I was alone in the dark with only the sound of the wind in the trees. I packed up camp and left.

The following summer, I traveled across country again, this time in a VW minibus, but I stuck to more populated areas: I'd learned. Too many trans people don't get off that easy.

What a Tangled Web We Weave . . .

In cultures, subcultures, and family units where disobedience or disregard for one's sex assigned at birth is considered an illness, it's an illness that can only be cured by silence. Here's how this one works: once we're taught that we are literally sick, that we have an illness that can be diagnosed and maybe cured, we've got to see therapists in order to receive the medical seal of approval required to proceed with any hormone therapy or gender reassignment surgery. We'll be cured, we're told, if we become members of one gender or another—and then only by means of surgery and hormones. On top of that, we are advised not to divulge our transgender status, except in select cases requiring intimacy. Isn't that amazing? When trans people present themselves for therapy in that kind of culture, we are channeled through a system that labels us as having a disease (transsexuality) for which the therapy is to lie, hide, or otherwise remain silent.

In the mid-'80s, I was told by several counselors and a number of transsexual peers that I would need to invent a past for myself as a little girl, that I'd have to make up incidents of my girl childhood; that I'd have to say things like, "When I was a little girl . . ." I never was a little girl; I'd lied all my life trying to be the boy, the man that I'd known myself **not** to be. Here I was, taking a giant step toward personal integrity by entering therapy with the truth and self-acknowledgment that I was a transsexual, and I was told, "Don't **tell** anyone you're transsexual."

What's more, in cultures, subcultures, and family units that insist on man-or-woman only, there's no opportunity for an individual to freely proclaim themselves to be nonbinary. Under these conditions, our therapy is to lie and say that we are men or women. This therapeutic lie is one reason that genderqueer, agender, nonbinary, and gender-nonconforming people haven't been saying too much about ourselves and our lives and our experience of gender; we're not allowed, in therapy, the right to think of ourselves as not-men, not-women.

This was where a different kind of therapy might have helped me. Perhaps if I hadn't spent so much time thinking and talking about being a woman, and perhaps if the psychiatrist who examined me had spent less time focusing on those aspects of my life which could never be changed by surgery, I would have had more opportunity to think about myself as a transsexual. It was exposure to the press that forced me to talk about my transsexuality, and it was a painful way to have to learn to do so.

—Caroline Cossey, My Story, 1992

Another reason for the silence of transsexuals lies in the mythology of transgender subculture. Two or more transgenders together, goes the myth, can be read more easily as trans—so they don't pass. I don't think that's it.

> In cases where trans people of different stripes don't get along, or stay away from each other, it's because we threaten the hell out of one another.

Each of us, transgender and cisgender, binary and nonbinary, develops a view of the world as we grow up—a view that validates our existence, gives us a reason for being, a justification for the nuttinesses that each of us might have. Most cisgender people (and many binary-identified trans people) have cultural norms on which to pin their worldview, reinforced by magazines, television, cinema, the internet, and the continually growing list of communications environments.

At this writing, trans folks in this culture are neither fairly nor accurately represented in the media, nor championed by a unified trans community, comprised of both binary- and nonbinary-identified trans folks. Growing up, our families rarely encourage us to pursue any questioning of gender. Before the internet, we had to develop our worldviews in solitude. Alone, we figured out why we're in the world the way we are. The early literature on the transgender experience did not help us to establish a truly transgender worldview in concert with other transgender people, because until quite recently, nearly all the books and theories about gender and transgender were written by cisgender folks who, no matter how well-intentioned, were each trying to figure out how to make us fit into *their* worldview. Now, given easy access to sites like Tumblr and YouTube, trans people do get to compare notes and worldviews. Even so, trans people learn to explain gender to themselves from a very early age.

When I was ten or eleven years old, I used to play alone in the basement, way back in the corner where no one would come along to disturb me. There was an old chair there to which I attached all manner of wires and boxes and dials: it was my gender-change machine. I would sit in that chair and twist the dials, and—presto—I was off on an adventure in my mind as a little girl, usually some budding dykelet like Nancy Drew or Pippi Longstocking.

Most transgender/transsexual people opt for the theory that there are men and women and no in-between ground: the agreed-upon gender system. That's what I did—I just knew I had to be one or the other—so, in my worldview, I saw myself as a mistake: some-*thing* that needed to be fixed and then placed neatly into one of two categories.

This isn't the case with nonbinary and gender-nonconforming trans folks. There's no data at this writing to determine the numbers of trans folks in binary and non-binary identities. But a stroll through the internet reveals some wonderfully subtle differences in the worldviews developed by individual trans folk of all stripes—binary and nonbinary alike. Talk to a few trans people and see how beautifully textured the normally drab concept of gender can become.

We bring our very personal explanations for our existence into contact with other trans people who have been spending *their* lives constructing their *own* reasons for existence. If, when we meet, our worldviews differ radically enough, we wind up threatening each other's basic understanding of the world—we threaten each other. So we'd rather not meet, we'd rather not talk. That's beginning to shift. Transgender and other trans people are finally sitting down, taking stock, comparing notes—and it's the dominant culture that's coming up short. Some of us are beginning to actually like ourselves and one another for the blend we are. Many of us are beginning to express our discontent with a culture that wants us silent.

> This Western culture of ours tends to sacrifice the full range of experience to a lower common denominator that's acceptable to more people; we end up with McDonald's instead of real food, Holiday Inns instead of homes, and **USA Today** instead of news and cultural analysis. And we do that with the rest of our lives. Our spirits are full of possibilities, yet we tie ourselves down to socially prescribed names and categories so we're acceptable to more people. We take on identities that no one has to think about, and that's probably how we become and why we remain men and women.

The first step in liberating ourselves from this meek-as-lambs culturally imposed silence is for trans people—binary and nonbinary alike—to begin talking with one another, asking one another sincere questions, and listening intently.

Myths and Myth-Conceptions

A great many trans subcultures are, at this writing, developing, and it's subsequently giving rise to new folktales and traditions of gender fluidity and ambiguity. For example:

» *We are the chosen people.*

> This is the point of view of many groups and religions, and is not the sole property of trans folks. This point of view reminds me of my days as a banner-waving Scientologist, and I usually disassociate myself from any group whose members proclaim some unique kinship to, or favored station with, some higher power.

» *We are normal men and women.*

> Okay, some of us are men and women. But who's to say that there is such a thing as a normal man or woman? I have this idea that there are only people who are fluidly gendered, and that the norm is that most people continually struggle to maintain the personal truth of being one gender or another. So if someone goes through a gender transition and then struggles to establish and maintain a (new) rigid gender, I guess that does make them normal. That's the only way I can see the grounding to this myth.

» *We are better men or women than men born men or women born women, because we had to work at it.*

I don't know about this one—I think everyone has to work at being a man or a woman. Transgender people are probably more aware of doing the work, that's all, and that does count for a lot. I'd say that transgender men and women are living their genders more mindfully than their cisgender counterparts. But the concept of some nebulously "better" class of people is not an idea of love and inclusion—rather, it's an idea of oppression.

» *We have an incurable disease.*

No, we don't.

» *We are trapped in the wrong body.*

I understand that many people may explain their preoperative transgender lives in this way, but I'll bet it's more likely an unfortunate metaphor that conveniently conforms to cultural expectations, rather than an honest reflection of our transgender feelings. As a people, we're short on metaphors, any metaphors, and when we find one that people understand, we stop looking. It's time for transgender people to look for new metaphors—new ways of communicating our lives to people who are traditionally gendered.

» *We are the most put-upon of people.*

Many marginalized people claim to be the least privileged and most at risk. Of course it's relative. At this writing, trans women of color are oppressed, denied, and at risk at nearly every level of the world's heirarchies. And still, it's important to maintain some perspective and apply a thorough, intersectional analysis before making a claim like that.

» *Drag queens are not trans.*

Trans may refer to *anyone* for whom the conscious management of their gender identity and/or expression takes up a significant part of their lives. By definition, that would include drag queens and drag kings (as well as cross-dressers, sissy men, and butch women). Some transgender women and men distance themselves from queens and kings by insisting that the latter are not transgender, i.e., men and women who've transitioned from another gender. But even that is not entirely true, because some drag performers are transgender and use drag as a means to finance their transitions— and some of those trans women and trans men continue performing drag after their transitions. My default assumption is that queens and kings (and sissies and butches and cross-dressers) are all part of my trans family. But the bottom line is that trans is a self-proclaimed identity in that you're trans if you own that you're trans—and no one is trans who doesn't own being trans.

» *There is a transgender community.*

*Someone asked me if the transgender community is like the lesbian/gay communities. I said no, because the lesbian/gay communities are based on who one relates to, whereas the transgender experience is different: it's about identity—relating to oneself. It's more an inward thing. When you have people together with **those** issues, the group dynamic is inherently very different.*

—David Harrison, in conversation
with the author, 1993

There are many trans communities, and yes, some of them are transgender. But trans communities crystalize and maintain themselves based on more factors than trans. There are so many out trans people these days that our communities are intersectional. There are trans communities that are based on race, faith, and politics. Trans people who work at the same company organize communities around their common employment. And there are communities that are based in the kind of trans we're talking about. There are transgender communities, nonbinary and genderqueer communities, and a good number of drag communities. And sure enough, David Harrison's observations on group dynamics (previous page) are visible in the differences between lesbian and gay group dynamics, and trans group dynamics. More and more, trans communities are integrating themselves into big-tent lesbian, gay, bisexual, and queer groups. Because of their differences in group dynamics, it's a tricky merger. And, bless their furry little activist hearts, they are really working hard at getting along. It's indicative, I think, of a slow shift from identity politics to intersectional politics.

There does exist an underground of male-to-female gender outlaws that already has its own unspoken hierarchy in relationship to their present mainstream culture, definable from whatever shoes you happen to be standing in—high heels or Reeboks.

> **Cisgender, binary-identified men and women:** Right, this is almost everybody, everywhere.
>
> What follows is a rough hierarchy of everyone else:
>
> **Binary-identified transgender men and women:** At this writing, this is the trans group that has reached a tipping point in mainstream culture. When people don't know much about us, this is who they think of when they hear the word **transgender**.

Within the transgender world, there's this hierarchy of respectability.

> **Postoperative:** Men and women who've had genital surgery and/or top surgery look down on:
>
> **Preoperative:** Men and women who've not yet had their genital and/or top surgery,

but they are planning on it. They in turn look down on:

Nonoperative: Men and women living in a gender identity opposite to their birth-assigned genders, but who have little or no intention of having genital and/or top surgery.

The majority of people who, for the most part, subscribe to a binary gender system consider their truth of gender to be more real than the truth of:

Out Cross-dressers and Transvestites: Usually heterosexual men who dress as they think women dress, and who are out in the open about doing that.

Nonbinary Trans People: People who just say no to a binary gender–defined life, and who understand themselves to be neither man nor woman, boy nor girl, male nor female. This includes androgynous or gender-nonconforming people who "look like" they are cisgender.

Queer-Identified Trans People: Can identify as trannies or not. By definition, queer defies hierarchy. Queer-identified trans folks are sometimes cis-appearing, sometimes male or female appearing, and less commonly gender-blended. So, in no particular order this includes people who identify as Fluidly Gendered, Genderqueers, Drag Queens, Ball Queens, Sissy men, Drag Kings, and Butch women. There are literally hundreds more queer identities. Thirty minutes with Google will bear me out.

She-Males, He-Shes, and Chicks with Dicks: A she-male friend of mine describes herself as "tits, big hair, lots of makeup, and a dick." These are fabulous individuals who for the most part work in adult entertainment, or as sex workers who are barely more respectable than . . .

Closet Cases: Men and women who hide their cross-dressing activities and often feel superior to transgender people, and so the hierarchy is an unbroken circle.

Keep in mind, all positions in this hierarchy of gender are subject and relative to race / ethnicity, age, class, sexuality, religion, disability, citizenship, geography, mental health, family and reproductive status, looks, language, legal status, and more. For example: In terms of looks, passing trans people live with more privilege than trans people who do not appear to the casual observer to fit neatly into male or female. People with visible and/or crippling disabilities live with far less recognition and privilege than their more able-bodied counterparts. Cisgender, binary-identified sex workers live with less access to public resources than most transgender people—binary and nonbinary—working in more mainstream professions. Cisgender men who are transamorous for trans women are at great risk for vilification and ridicule. The degree to which a person's sexuality is considered kinky—or is expressed loudly, proudly, and/or flamboyantly—greatly impacts a person's rights and respectability. And of course race impacts the freedom of trans people as much as it impacts cis people.

All recognitions, privileges, and access to what should be public resources are relative to cultural or familial context and point of view.

Most transmasculine-identified groups, as well as some working-class transgender organizations I've been associated with, have been more inclusive in their membership and attendance requirements than groups whose memberships are mostly middle-class, mostly white, and mostly transfeminine-identified. They're also less hierarchical in both their meeting procedure and ways of relating to one another. Very few groups exist, however, that encompass the full rainbow that is gender outlawism, and sadly, groups still divide along the lines of male-to-female and female-to-male gender outlaws.

We are all longing to go home to some place we have never been—a place, half-remembered, and half-envisioned, we can only catch glimpses of from time to time. Community. Somewhere, there are people to whom we can speak with passion without having the words catch in our throats. Somewhere a circle of hands will open to receive us, eyes will light up as we enter, voices will celebrate with us whenever we come into our own power. Community means strength that joins our strength to do the work that needs to be done. Arms to hold us when we falter. A circle of healing. A circle of friends. Someplace where we can be free.

—*Starhawk*, Dreaming the Dark: Magic, Sex, and Politics, 1982

I'd like to be a member of a community some day. One of the reasons I didn't go through with my gender change for such a long time was the certain knowledge that I would be an outsider, and considered to be a freak. All trans-identified people find a common ground in that we each break one or more of the rules of gender. Whether we enjoy the moniker or not, what we have in common is that we are all viewed in mainstream culture as gender outlaws, every one of us. Some of us fight that cultural attribution, and some of us embrace it. To attempt to divide us into rigid categories ("**You're** a transvestite, and **you're** a drag queen, and **you're** a she-male," and on and on and on) is like trying to apply the laws of solids to the state of fluids: it's our fluidity that keeps us in touch with one another. It's our fluidity and the principles that attend that constant state of flux that could create an innovative and inclusive trans community.

I really *would* like to be a member of a trans community, but until there's one that's based on the principle of constant change, the membership would involve more rules, and rules around the subject of gender are not rules I want to obey.

The Fly, the leader of a gang of criminals in the Wilma Theater production of the Brecht/Weill musical Happy End, *1987, in Philadelphia, directed by Jiri Zizka. It was my first role in women's clothing, and I doubled as the male master of ceremonies.*

8

GENDER TERROR, GENDER RAGE

*If transsexuality marks a response to the dream of changing sex, it is also clearly the object of dreaming, and even phantasizing, in non-transsexuals. In the final analysis, sexual difference, which owes much to symbolic dualisms, belongs to the register of the **real**. It constitutes an insuperable barrier, an irreducible wall against which one can bang one's head indefinitely.*

—Catherine Millot, Horsexe/Essays on
Transexuality, 1990

For a while, I thought that it would be fun to call what I do in life gender terrorism. Seemed right at first—I and so many folks like me were terrorizing the structure of gender itself. But I've come to see it a bit differently now—gender terrorists are not the drag queens, the butch dykes, the men on roller skates dressed as nuns. Gender terrorists are not the female-to-male transsexual who's learning to look people in the eyes while he walks down the street. Gender terrorists are not the leather daddies or backseat Betties. Gender terrorists are not the married men, shivering in the dark as they slip on their wives' panties. Gender terrorists are those who, like Ms. Millot, bang their heads against a gender system that to them is real and natural; and who then use gender to terrorize the rest of us. These are the real terrorists: the Gender Defenders.

[A]nything that undermines confidence in the scheme of classification on which people base their lives sickens them as though the very ground on which they stood precipitously dropped away. The vertigo produced by the loss of cognitive orientation is similar to that produced by the loss of physical orientation. Philosophic nausea, certain forms of schizophrenia, moral revulsion, negative experience, the horror of having violated a taboo, and the feeling of having been polluted are all manifestations of this mental **mal de mer***, occasioned by the sudden shipwreck of cognitive orientation which casts one adrift in a world without structure.*

People will regard any phenomenon that produces this disorientation as "disgusting" or "dirty." To be so regarded, however, the phenomenon must threaten to destroy not only one of their fundamental cognitive categories but their whole cognitive system.

—Murray S. Davis, Smut: Erotic
Reality/Obscene Ideology, 1983

That's what gender outlaws do: our mere presence is often enough to make people sick. Take that great scene in the classic 1992 film *The Crying Game*. You know the scene: the one that got all the attention—the one you weren't supposed to talk about? The one with the (gasp) full penile nudity—on the body of what appeared to be a woman! To me, the telling aspect of the scene is not so much the revelation of the person as trans as much as it was the nausea and vomiting by the guy who did the discovering. That's a fairly strong reaction in any language, any culture. That's disgust, pure and simple. Many trans people will tell you that's an all-too-accurate reaction; one usually followed, as in *The Crying Game*, by a physical attack on the trans person. With all the talk centering on the movie at the time of its release, no one focused on the issue of disgust. I think no one brought it up, because it would draw focus to the other side of revulsion: desire. The revelation of Dil's gender ambiguity calls into question both the sexual orientation (desire) and the gender identity of Fergus.

> Fergus's inner dialogue may have gone like this: "I'm really turned on by this woman, and that's how it should be—I'm male and I'm heterosexual." Then, as Dil disrobes, that inner voice might protest, "Wait! She's got a penis! She's a man!" And then the real awful truth may reveal itself like this: "Wait, I'm still attracted to this person, this man! But only women and faggots go for men—does that mean I'm a woman? Does it mean I'm homosexual?"
> Poor baby!

His vomiting can be seen not so much as a sign of revulsion as an admission of desire and attraction, and the consequential upheaval of his gender identity and sexual orientation. The questioning of these heretofore unquestioned states of very personal identity would certainly result in nausea—the poor man's cognitive system had really been shaken up! I don't think *The Crying*

Game is saying it's good to throw up when you find out someone is trans; I think the movie is brilliantly showing us that it's sadly a common response.

And how about the public silence surrounding *The Crying Game* when it was released in 1992? No one wanted to give away the "big secret." The last time there was such a furor about "don't give away the surprise ending," it was Hitchcock's 1960 film *Psycho* . . . and the surprise was: another trans person. The public response of "don't say a word" is more than "don't spoil the movie." What's to spoil, anyway? I knew about "the secret" before I went, and I thoroughly enjoyed the film. No, I think the "keep the secret" response on the part of the public was more a reflection of how the Gender Defenders of this culture would like to see trans people: as a secret, hidden away from public view.

> A Gender Defender is someone who actively, or by knowing inaction, defends the status quo of the binary gender system, and thus perpetuates the violence of male privilege and all its social extensions. A Gender Defender, or gender terrorist, is someone for whom binary gender forms a cornerstone of their view of the world. Shake gender up for one of these folks, and you're in for trouble. At this writing, nowhere is this more evident than in all the furor in the United States over gender-segregated bathrooms.

What Are They Afraid Of?

Because gender ambiguity and gender outlaws are just now making themselves visible in the world, the defenders of gender rigidity lash out at the nearest familiar labels: homosexuality and lesbianism, the points at which gender outsiders intersect with sexual outsiders. And so, transphobia and homophobia become conflated.

> **Transphobia** is one heck of an interesting word. Fear of crossing? Fear of transgressing? If this term were allowed **that** sort of breadth—that is, including the fear and hatred of **any** kind of binary-breakers—then the fear of trans people becomes well contextualized within the fear of crossing borders.

The acts of a Gender Defender are acts of violence against gender outsiders.

» Gay bashing is one act of Gender Defenders.

> » Have you seen a single gay man or lesbian walking down the street recently?
> » How did you know or why did you suspect that they were gay or lesbian?
> » Was it something they were doing sexually? Or something about their gender expression?
> » Why do gay bashers pick out certain gays and lesbians to bash?

» The attack on transsexuals by some trans-excluding radical feminists is simply another defense of gender.

All transsexuals rape women's bodies by reducing the real female form to an artifact, appropriating this body for themselves. However, the transsexually constructed lesbian-feminist violates women's sexuality and spirit, as well. Rape, although it is usually done by force, can also be accomplished by deception. It is significant that in the case of the transsexually constructed lesbian-feminist, often he is able to gain entrance and a dominant position in women's spaces because the women involved do not know he is a transsexual and he just does not happen to mention it.

—Janice G. Raymond,
The Transsexual Empire, 1979

Both Raymond and Millot generalize beyond what would be acceptable practice in any academic work; that's a mark of their fanaticism. But there's some historical, cross-cultural precedent for their concern that trans people are bad for feminism: the Navajo *nadle*. The *nadle* is a sort of transgender male-to-female person, with a unique social function: the *nadle* was often called upon to suppress the women's revolutions. Neither Raymond nor Millot seem familiar with these wolves in chic clothing, but both implicitly fear the concept.

*The **nadle***'s role and value in mythology are male-oriented. Barren themselves, the **nadle** are useful as mediators, and, perhaps related to this, they serve as ferrymen. When there was a quarrel between the men and the women and the latter secluded themselves on one side* *of the river, the* **nadle**, *by deciding to bring the women back across, enabled the men to overcome the women. In doing this, they acted as [gender] strikebreakers or scabs, reversing the course of the age-old theme of the strike of one [gender] against the other.*

—Wendy O'Flaherty, Women, Androgynes,
and Other Mythical Beasts, 1980

I've seen some examples of what Raymond fears: male-to-female transsexuals entering "women-only" spaces and attempting to assume positions of control and power. If Raymond herself has personally experienced that, I can empathize with her anger—she and others are of the mistaken belief that "women only" means the same thing to everyone as it means to them. My contention, however, is that it is not the trans person or even the issue of transgender that is bad for feminism: I think that what's bad for the future of feminism is male privilege, and I think that occasionally a male-to-female transsexual will carry more than a small degree of that over into their newly gendered life. A better solution to this situation would be to point out what's going on, and to talk it through. I don't think unconsciously wielded privilege of any kind has a place *anywhere*, and I think it would best be processed out of *any* environment.

Raymond and her supporters bring up the subject of deception. Personally, I agree that hiding, and not proclaiming one's trans status, is an unworthy stance—even a heinous act—if one's invisible status is maintained with the purpose of gaining power. Trans women are moving, however, in the direction of openly embracing—either willingly, or by the probing eye of public interest—a more nuanced gender identity as women.

» Segments of the men's movement defend gender.

I'm talking about men who drum and chant in the woods to ward off the possibility of being called women. What's amusing is that lesbians had been drumming and chanting in the woods for well over a decade before Robert Bly and company got the bright idea to appropriate the practice and proclaim it "male."

» Legislating who gets to use which bathrooms, locker rooms, and other binary-gendered spaces is the act of a Gender Defender.

[Regarding] Single-Sex Multiple Occupancy Bathroom and Changing Facilities: Public agencies shall require every multiple occupancy bathroom or changing facility to be designated for and only used by persons based on their biological sex.

(1) Biological sex: The physical condition of being male or female, which is stated on a person's birth certificate.

—General Assembly of North Carolina Second Extra Session 2016, House Bill 2

I just bet that some brave and mischievous lawyer is going to have a lot of fun parsing in court "the physical condition of being male or female" beyond penis-or-no-penis. And are trans people really that much of a threat to traditionally gendered people? I think a lot of folks have underrated Gore Vidal's **Myra Breckinridge,** and the sequel **Myron.** In fact, the movie version of **Myra Breckinridge** has been called one of the worst movies of all time. I think it has a lot to do with the point Vidal makes: that the sort of trans people who exist sexually for pleasure, and not procreation, strike terror at the heart of our puritanical Eurocentric culture. Vidal positions Myra as the voice and agent of doom for the traditional American male—aka "the real man." I think he was on the mark, and I'm proud to call Myra my sister.

The Protection Racket

We can feel secure in the protection provided by a group, but that protection has its **price**. *Compliance with the group often extends further than acceptance of the group's views to include* **participation** *in the attack on deviants by subtle (or not so subtle) disapproval, punishment, or rejection of any member who voices criticism of the consensus. . . . [The] dissident is criticized as disloyal, lacking commitment, interfering with the important work of the group.*

—Arthur J. Deikman, The Wrong Way Home: Uncovering Patterns of Cult Behavior in American Society, 1990

Protection for trans people is only now entering the legal canon. As of yet, there is no group dynamic strong enough to ward off possible attacks on individuals. I'm not looking forward to the policeman's baton, the media's poison, or the assassin's bullet—sadly, these are almost inevitable in this at once thrilling and dangerous world of wave after wave of marginalized peoples surging to the center of mainstream culture, confronting the dominant ideology.

This culture attacks people on the basis of being or not being correctly gendered (having—and appearing to have—a politically correct body). It's when we get to a point of knowing we're not gendered in the same way as our friends, relatives, and co-workers—it's then that we get angry and start to do something about gender.

» What's your gender?
» When did you first realize that you are that gender?
» How much say do you have in your gender?
» Is there anything about your gender or gender role that you don't like, or that gets in your way?
» Are there one or two qualities about another gender that are appealing to you, enough so that you'd like to incorporate those qualities into your daily life?
» What would happen to your life if you did that?
» What would your gender be then?

> » How do you think people would respond to you?
> » How would you feel if they did that?

Gender Activism Begins with Gender Rage

Penguin: "You're just jealous because **I'm** *a real freak, and* **you** *have to wear a mask!"*
Batman: "You just may be right."
>   —*Tim Burton,* Batman Returns, *1993*

> Sometimes, it's not the fist in your belly that
>   gets to you.
> Sometimes, it's when they're quiet, even
>   polite.
> Sometimes, it's how they look at you day
>   after day that finally gets to you.
> They squint at you, like they can't see.
> It's as if by squinting
>   they might bring you into better focus.
> If they're in a crowd, they shift their eyes
>   so their friends can't tell they're looking
>   at you.
>   Real subtle.
> You can read the fear behind the smirk,
> The hatred just past the disgust.
> You worry it's your paranoia.
> And you always hope it's only your paranoia.
> (Confidence, they've told you, helps you
>   pass.)
> But there's always one of them who looks
>   at you with longing.

And that scares you the most,
Because if you let that longing into your
heart, you have to accept yourself
just the way you are.

It's not only people who intentionally transgress gender who get into trouble. Eventually the gender system lets everyone down. It seems to be rigged that way. Sometimes, even with all the time and effort we put into obeying the rules, we get hurt. We can get badly hurt by being a real man or a real woman.

So what happens to the person who finds out that they have been duped or disappointed by some aspect of gender? How does someone come to terms with some inner ambiguity of gender, and the demands of a rigid, nearly monolithic, universal binary gender system? This person could get closer to the gender outlaws who have previously been regarded as outsiders. This person would sense some common ground with the more obvious renegades of the gender system, usually some commonality in the area of gender role oppression. Bridging the gap between themself and the outlaws, these former Gender Defenders can't devalue the outsider without devaluing themselves. Instead of someone defending gender, we've now got someone who begins intentionally to bend gender, if only by their acceptance of those who are openly bending the rules of binary gender.

> » What are you being denied on account of your gender?
> » What does a person of another gender have that you can't have?

And this brings up a great deal of anger. Because, we've suddenly positioned ourselves in the area previously marked "freaks only." We've chosen to stand with the marginalized. But standing with freaks never hurt anyone—it's when we agree that we deserve the oppression and the ridicule that accompanies the freak's position in the culture—that's when the wound is mortal.

> The first national television show I did was **The Geraldo Rivera Show**. The subject was **Transsexual Regrets: Who's Sorry Now?** It was supposed to be about all these transsexuals who'd gotten fairly far along in their transition but were now changing their minds. I was there with psychologist Jayne Thomas to provide a little balance: we were the happy transsexuals. Somewhere around the time when an audience member asked me if I could "orgasm with that vagina," I realized that yep, I was a freak all right, but I was only a freak to the degree that I remained silent. When I spoke, I had a chance to educate, and, paradoxically, I became less of a freak.

We don't deserve the ridicule, the stares, the fist in our bellies. We are entitled to our anger in response to this oppression: our anger is a message to ourselves that we need to get active and change something in order to survive. So we resist the oppression, the violence—we resist the tendency of the culture to see us as a joke.

So now we're standing on the side of the freaks. Now what? If we can't call the freaks names anymore because we realize we're one of them, then we have to look back at our position as a former insider, and we begin to devalue *that*. We've now officially become activists. But outside or inside, it's still a side; and taking a side usually means taking the identity of a side, and there you have identity politics as one more rendering of a game called us-versus-them. In trans politics, as in any other identity politics, *we* look around for a *them*. From the standpoint of the trans person, there's no shortage of *them*, no shortage at all. It just makes me sad that we continually cast other trans people whose truth of trans differs from our own as "them."

A theater critic for the **San Francisco Chronicle** once chided me for bringing a show about transsexualism to a lesbian and gay theater. "Preaching to the converted," he called it. Who or what did he think was in the audience? I tell you, I **wish** there had been an audience of transsexuals out there each night! I'd have felt a lot less lonely and vulnerable than I did. People make assumptions.

Loose Canons of Activism

One trouble in having only a few of *us* and a lot of *them* is that it's easy to hit out at the wrong *them*. Over the past few decades, some transgender activists have targeted trans-excluding radical feminists because these women have established something called "women-only" spaces; and a small number of these women will not brook the admission of trans women, whom the separatists don't acknowledge to be women. In response to demands for inclusion by the trans women, the cis women on the inside get angry and a war of epithets begins. It's a war about who's a man and who's a woman. It's the same war that's being fought on the battlefield of bio sex–segregated bathrooms. But there's a big difference.

From what I can see, women inhabit "women-only" spaces to heal from the oppression of their number by the larger culture, by men in particular, and because they don't see us as women, we're perceived as the other side of the binary: men. Perceived as men, we get in the way of their healing, and so we're excluded.

> The current phraseology is "women born women." We're told that only "women born women" are allowed into some space. Well, that's a problem. Aside from the obvious absurdity of a newborn infant being called a woman, the phrase "woman born woman" just throws us back into the what's-a-woman question.

Some trans women take exclusion by lesbian separatists as oppression, but I don't think so. Lesbian *oppression* at the hands of the dominant ideology is not the same as the *exclusion* experienced by trans women at the hands of the lesbian separatists. Most lesbian activists just don't have the same economic and social resources with which to oppress trans women. I think both sides need to sit down and talk with each other, and I think both sides need to do some serious listening.

> I once stated this opinion in a San Francisco newspaper article. A small number of transgender activists called me a Nazi and a reactionary, and claimed I'd set "the cause" back years through that article. Their accusation was that I was giving fuel to "the enemy." I got harassing phone calls, and they threatened to demonstrate against my next theater piece. Like I said, I don't speak for all trans people.

A free society is one where it is safe to
be unpopular.

—*Adlai Stevenson*

I think that anger and activism mix about as well as drinking and driving. When I'm angry, I don't have the judgment to select a correct target to hit out against. I do believe that anger is healthy, that it can lead to a recognition of the *need* for action, but activism itself is best accomplished by level heads who can help steer others' anger toward correct targets. A correct target is the group that has both the will and the power to oppress you wherever you go. The correct target for any successful trans rebellion would be the gender system itself, and many trans people are doing just that. But trans men and women won't attack that system until they themselves are free of the need to participate in it.

Trans is the first marginalized activism to form itself and grow up in the early days of the internet. Maybe the instantaneous widespread communication that comes with the internet will preclude the need for a full-on physical rebellion. I sure hope so. Because in the past, social reform movements have tended to coalesce around a particular moment of rebellion. A unified trans moment of rebellion has not yet come, but trans people are growing more and more restless.

And look, the trans Stonewall or Selma, Alabama, is not going to come about by attacking members of our own trans family. And it won't be a rebellion if trans people attack gays and lesbians—even lesbian separatists, who are clearly gender outlaws like ourselves. In Selma, and at the Stonewall, members of marginalized groups resorted to urban warfare in order to stand up to the more tangible force of oppression: the police state. It is my most sincere wish that trans activism will coalesce without bloodshed.

It does hurt, being attacked or even excluded by other marginalized groups, and that makes me feel a shame I thought I'd gotten over a long time ago. It's not what people say when they exclude me and my people, or how they say it, but rather it's a very long ache that I don't believe will stop until there's a whole lot more room in the world for difference. Sometimes it's a seemingly insignificant act of exclusion that will tip the scale and turn someone from insider to outsider, like the one that really got to me. It was a bathroom moment, my first experience with what theorist Marjorie Garber calls urinary segregation.

When I first went through my gender change, I was working for an IBM subsidiary in Philadelphia. The biggest quandary there was "Which bathroom is it going to use?" To their credit, most of the people in my office didn't really care; it was the building manager who was tearing his hair out over this one. I suppose he felt I would terrorize the women in their bathroom, and lie in waiting for the men in **their** bathroom. Finally, a solution was reached: even though I worked on the eleventh floor of a large office building, I would use a bathroom on the seventh floor. The seventh floor had been under construction, but for lack of funds they simply stopped construction;

no one worked on that floor. Piles of plaster and wiring littered the floor, and pools of water lay everywhere. But there was a working bathroom in the very back of that floor, and that's where they sent me. No one ever cleaned it, no one kept it stocked. It was poorly lit and it was scary. Isn't it amazing the lengths we'll go to in order to maintain the illusion that there are only two genders, and that these genders must remain separate? Most gender outlaws have some similar bathroom horror story.

Something happens, some final bit that lights up the injustice of the binary gender system, and in that flash, we see that the emperor is wearing no clothes. That this either/or gender system we've got is truly oppressing us. That happens, and we snap; we begin to fight.

» Have you ever been teased or baited by reason of acting outside your assigned gender role?
» Where do you think the sanctions for that teasing or baiting come from?

There are a lot of ways to fight, and trans people are just now coming together in the common fight for the right to express our genders freely. Where once we met only in drag bars or someone else's pride marches, we're now meeting in our own protest marches and in Facebook groups.

» Would you like to meet other people who feel the same way you do about gender?

» Would you like to hear you're not the only one?
» Would you like to know you've got a history in this world?
» Do you think that might make you smile?

We meet to discuss ways and means of securing our freedom. In this quest for our freedom of identity and expression, there comes a point where the binary gender system reveals itself to be not only oppressive but silly. When we see how ridiculous it is, we can truly begin to dismantle it.

Pay close attention to your political enemies, especially the smart ones. Then figure out how to make them laugh.

—John Waters, addressing the class of 2016,
Rhode Island School of Design

The Marquis de Sade in the 1969 Brown University production of **Marat/Sade,** directed by John Emigh.

9

SEND IN THE CLOWNS

A few weeks after I told my mother that I was going to become her daughter, she phoned me with a question: "Are you sure," she asked, "this change of yours isn't just another role? You've always been an actor, is this just another part, maybe your most challenging one?" At the time, I was offended. How dare she, I asked myself, compare my life's struggle with some part in a play?! But, looking back, it really was a good question. Thanks, Mom.

Real gender freedom begins with fun. Honest. Really. I mean, why do it if it's not going to be fun? I know that saying something is fun in today's world devalues, demeans, and diminishes whatever it is that we think is fun. But that only happens in someone *else's* eyes. To those of us having the fun that comes with gender freedom—hell, nothing can diminish the value and importance of that.

The Gender Blender is a sort of whirling confusion of leather and rhinestones. Some cultures call them street fairies, some cultures call them genderqueer—names change. But whatever they are called, they are mindfully and fabulously mixing up gender. These creatures do not spring full-born from the forehead of the culture; they earn their feather boa wings step by step, feather by feather.

> In contrast, the majority of binary identified trans people express themselves more conservatively. Shifting one's gender expression is a learning process. It's easy to spot someone who's learning a new gender: they move just a bit slower than most people; he or she is unlearning old ways of moving, and picking up new ways of moving. So one of the first things you try to do is to move at a normal pace, because you don't want to be laughed at. You don't want the high school kids pointing and yelling. You don't want to see the looks of disgust on people's faces. So you learn how to blend in. It's called "passing."

[The stand-up comic] seems to know no fear of humiliation and thus appears to be dangerously outside the boundaries of social control.
        —David Marc, "Comic Visions: Television Comedy and American Culture," 1989

Humiliation is a whip of the defenders of gender. Humiliation of the other is sanctioned at virtually every level of the culture. It's only recently become politically incorrect to laugh at binary-identified trans people. People still do it, but it's frowned upon in more progressive circles. Generally speaking, people are still allowed to laugh at a nonbinary-identified person. But nonbinary folks are beginning to learn that when there's no fear of being humiliated for one's portrayal of gender, there's less opportunity for the culture to exert control.

> I was on my way to a surgeon's office on the Upper East Side. It was rush hour, and the train station was packed. There was a large crowd of people avoiding an old man who was standing in the middle of the passageway. I heard his voice up ahead, above the noise of the crowd.
>
> "Sir, twenty-five cents, please."
>
> Or he'd say, "Lady, got a quarter?"
>
> I was reaching into my bag for some change, just as the motion of the crowd brought me face-to-face with him.
>
> He was so grimy.
>
> He stank of urine and wine.
>
> He looked right at me.
>
> "Lady?" he said.
>
> "Mister?" he said.
>
> "Say, what the fuck are you?" he said. And he began to laugh.
>
> He laughed. And he laughed. He just laughed. And the crowd carried me farther down the passageway, and I could still hear him laughing.

We're taught to heed the message, because it can be enforced by violence, the other whip of the system. Permissible and even institutionalized violence against trans people—just like the permissible and institutionalized violence against people of color—makes freedom from the fear of humiliation tricky, to say the least. And violence is more likely when a person embodies outsider status in both gender and race. So you have some choices: you can get real good at hiding, or you can get beat up. You can commit suicide. Or you learn how to laugh, and make others laugh. Please do stay alive. There are actually quite a few opportunities for everyone to laugh, but fear keeps us from looking at those opportunities. Cross-culturally, the individuals who have freed themselves from the fear of humiliation are clowns, fools, jesters, and tricksters. This can be Coyote, Uncle Tolpa, Br'er Rabbit, Raccoon Dog, or any number of documented practitioners of what Scoop Nisker calls *crazy wisdom* in cultures around the world.

The great fool, like Einstein, wonders about the obvious and stands in awe of the ordinary, which makes him capable of revolutionary discoveries about space and time. The great fool lives outside the blinding circle of routine, remaining open to the surprise of each moment. We are the foolish ones, complacent in our understanding. We take for granted the miraculous dance of creation, but the great fool continuously sees it for the first time. The revelations of the great fool often show us where we are going, or—more often—where we are.

—*Scoop Nisker,* Crazy Wisdom, *1990*

What do fools have in common? Well, they break the rules, they laugh at most rules, and they encourage us to laugh at ourselves. Their pranks of substituting one thing for another create instability and uncertainty, making visible the lies embedded in a culture. Fools demonstrate the wisdom of simplicity and innocence. These are valuable crafts, these are skills we could use in our problem-laden world.

I had the great good fortune to accompany Caitlyn Jenner and company as a regular cast member of E! TV's reality series *I Am Cait*. It was one of the very best times of my life. I remember at one point, Caitlyn Jenner was defending her right-wing politics to several of us, saying that if a right-winger ever ended up as president of the United States, she, Caitlyn, would be in a great position to be that president's trans ambassador. Well, that made me think. And think. And think. And about a week later, I announced my solidarity with CJ, saying I would be in a great position to be that Republican president's court jester.

The market value of comedy ascends in the face of a plausible end to history.
—*David Marc, "Comic Visions: Television Comedy and American Culture,"* 1989

Any healthy civilization would certainly have people performing these fool skills at every level of the culture. In *our* civilization, the only people doing these things are considered troublemakers, whatever their line of work.

The only true art is art that raises questions and implicates people.
—*Holly Hughes,*
Sphinxes Without Secrets, 1990

There's both room and need in our Eurocentric culture for a social class of clowns, jesters, tricksters, and fools. In fact, there are a lot of positions open. Since very few people are volunteering, since people laugh at us anyway, and since we have such wit, charm, and impeccable fashion sense, I think nonbinary trans people should move right into these roles.

> I mentioned this once in writing, and it raised the question of how does someone who's not an actor or a writer, and who (sensibly) doesn't want to **be** an actor or a writer, get along in this role. I think it's just a matter of incorporating a sense of humor into our daily lives. I think it has a lot to do with taking the tendency people have for laughing at us, and laughing **first**, so as to highlight and defuse that mechanism. That doesn't take talent; it takes living life at one's right size. It takes an admission of one's outsider status, and a wish to help others expand their points of view. It takes compassion.

Who Are the Fools?

The fool's role can be taken on at the office administrator's desk as easily as on the stage. The clown can perform in a circus or on a bus. The jester can take the ear of a king, or the ear of a neighbor. The trickster can fool the Congress of the United States, or their followers on social media. Today's more widely known fools are the solo performers, monologuists, stand-ups, anyone who addresses or performs before any audience, like the odd instructor or professor. You can go online and find any number of marvelous gender-blending fools on Tumblr or YouTube. These folks are the twenty-first century's answer to the roving minstrel or countryside jester. And there were some marvelous fools back at the turn of the century—Gender Blenders like these friends of mine:

» **Sandy Stone**, singled out for attack by Janice Raymond in her book *The Transsexual Empire*, in 1979. After a dozen years of recovery and research, Stone is once more back on the scene with her rib-tickling, devilish essay "The Empire Strikes Back: A Posttranssexual Manifesto." You can easily find it online via a search on the title.

» **Elvis Herselvis**, a San Francisco–based lesbian writer and Elvis impersonator; and

» **Glamoretta Rampage**, an early incarnation of author, actress, chanteuse, and bonne vivante Mx. Justin Vivian Bond. Go ahead, plug their names into a YouTube search. You will be so happy you did.

» **Shelly Mars**, performance artist and drag king extraordinaire from New York City.

» The late writer/director **Ingrid Wilhite**, whose two films, *Fun with a Sausage* and *The Mister Sisters*, lovingly lampoon the limits of lesbian identity and nicely blur the lines of gender identity and sexual orientation.

» **The Sisters of Perpetual Indulgence, Inc.**, is, per their literature, "a controversial order of gay, bisexual, and transgender 'nuns' of various religious backgrounds founded in Iowa in the mid-1970s." The Sisters hold various fund-raising events to benefit various AIDS-related groups.

SISTER SAM WANTS YOU!
JOIN QUEER ARMY TODAY!
NO WARS—FABULOUS PARADES!
—From a recruitment flyer for
the Sisters of Perpetual Indulgence, 1992

» The late **Doris Fish**, Australia and San Francisco; the late **'Tippi,'** San Francisco; the late **Ethyl Eichelberger**, New York: three transgendered performance artists with AIDS who died within a year of one another.

Today, the most well-known Gender Blenders are the drag queen superstars like RuPaul, Jinkx Monsoon, and Alaska Thunderfuck. I used to think that drag performance was a gimmick, a shtick, an appropriation; that life as a drag queen or drag king is different, less radical even than living a binary-identified trans life, because the latter is "full-time." Well yes, trans women and trans men are devotedly and mindfully living in a gender they were not assigned at birth. That's a hell of a change. But after a few years, that stops being a change and living in that other gender becomes more and more comfortable, less of a change. In contrast, most queens live out of drag as effeminate men—and that's a gender almost everyone picks on. So a drag queen spends their life changing from queen to sissy to queen to sissy to queen to sissy. That's not full-time? That's not radical? I'm not brave enough to live like that. How about you?

These days, both drag queens and trans women rightfully insist that they are unique and separate identities. But trans women don't want to be seen as drag queens. And many queens have too much fun as gay boys and don't want to be saddled 24/7 with their drag persona. What's more, some trans women love to perform in drag. And some drag queens know themselves to be trans women—drag is how they're making a living until they can move forward into their transition. By the same token, some trans men and butch dykes often share the same taste in masculine clothing—theirs are unique gender identities, with similar gender expressions. To the unschooled eye, drag queens and trans women look alike, as may drag kings and butch dykes. Oh, the fireworks that can result from *that* misgendering!

All that said, there's a big difference between performing gender for an audience and performing gender in day-to-day life. The contrast between trans as life and trans with a showbiz component marks one major difference between mainstream theater and what might be called queer theater. Back in the days before there was a respectable LGBT presence in mainstream media, we performed our outsider lives onstage—we bragged about them, we kidded about them. There was a strength in knowing we had our own comics, our own jokers.

But here it gets tricky. The pressure and temptation is to create art or politics for a particular group, which is in turn based on some inflexible identity: special interest groups, identity politics, whatever you want to call it. The group becomes loyal audience, supporters, and followers, if for no other reason than the fool is speaking their language, performing their lives.

But this is so important: the fool became a fool by flexing the rules, the boundaries of the group, and this is antithetical to the survival dynamic of most groups. A group remains a group by being inflexible: once it stretches its borders, it's no longer the same group. A fool, in order to survive, must not identify long with any rigidly structured group. When more and more of the fool's work is done for a particular identity-based group, then the fool becomes identified with the group. The fool is indeed foolish who serves a special interest, and will quickly cease being a fool.

So where do all these transgender fools go, if not to lead or participate in some grand and glorious transgender revolution? They climb yet another step on the ladder of transgender evolution: they move toward some spiritual awareness and practice.

We must never forget that art is not a form of propaganda, it is a form of truth.
                    —John Fitzgerald Kennedy

10

FIRST YOU DIE, AND THEN YOU GET THEIR ATTENTION

There are fools, there are damn fools, and there are great fools. Where a fool might color inside the lines of gender, a damn fool might blur the lines—and a great fool sees no lines at all. To the great fool, or holy fool, or shaman, there is no us-versus-them— we are at once uniquely individual and united. The great fool, or shaman, could be called a Gender Transcender.

Gender enlightenment begins with death. The shaman, cross-culturally, is someone who dies (literally or figuratively), has a brush with the spirit world, and returns to this world. There can be all sorts of death for the shaman.

> The night before my genital surgery, I cut myself. I used to wear a small labrys around my neck. It's a double-headed ax, a symbol of goddess culture reputedly popular with Amazon warriors. I cut myself lightly across my left wrist with one blade and above my heart with the other blade. I was killing that part of me I considered to be a man. This was the final blow; it was my personal ritual. The next morning, I was given a shot of antihistamine to calm me down and to stop me from dripping from places that might be

inconvenient to the surgeon. I was placed on the surgical cart and wheeled into the operating room. Lying on my back, I could only see the lights in the ceiling going by one by one. I remembered lying on some roughly hewn cart, staring upward at the sun and the sky. Inside the operating room, the nurse anesthesiologist gave me another shot and told me to count backward from one hundred. I got to ninety-six and then I died.

I woke up once during the procedure: I felt a sharp pain in what had once been my left testicle. Some more anesthesia, and I was dead again.

When I was very young, I would pray each night to wake up and be a girl. I'd add that part at the end of "Now I lay me down to sleep . . ." I remember waking from death back in my hospital bed and realizing that my old childhood prayer had come true. I reached for my tarot deck and selected a card at random—ace of cups: happiness.

What's said to happen in the instant/eternity between death and rebirth is that the spirits give the shaman a portion of the truth to take back to this world—a tiny grain of sand from the vast beaches of universal truth. But there's a catch. The shaman can hang on to that portion of the truth only if they tell it to others. If the shaman fails to reveal that portion of the truth continually to others, then the shaman is driven mad by the spirits.

This all sounded fairly esoteric until I put it into the terms of my very un-esoteric life. I died a virtual death, not only on the operating table but in terms of a key aspect of my identity, and then I was reborn into the world. For me, the in-between place itself was the truth I was made aware of, the existence of a place that lies outside the borders of what's culturally acceptable.

But here's the kicker: I was born into the twentieth-century world that used to tell people like me to be silent, to not reveal that I'm transsexual, to not reveal my truth. It was the old therapeutic lie that eventually caused me/us to go mad. Fortunately, very few therapists today counsel us to hide. It's hiding, passing, and being silent that makes me/us crazy. Silence does equal death—that principle applies to any situation involving a culturally mandated silence, and it's important to observe the neither/nor middle-space phenomenon of the shaman in any virtual death/rebirth situation. There's a portion of life's great truths that can be learned in that space.

The shamanic model can be seen in the sobering-up of an alcoholic—which would account for the importance that recovering alcoholics place on telling their stories. And if we don't tell our stories, we fall off the wagon, or we go mad. The shamanic phenomenon can be heard in the coming-out story of a lesbian woman or gay man. Have you noticed that shortly after making friends with a lesbian or gay man, they tell you their coming-out story? And that goes for anyone who identifies as out on the margins of sexuality and gender. They shifted from one space to another, and crossed some middle ground. Then, at some point, they came out to themselves and those dear to them. Their portion of the world's truth is somewhere in that story.

Sometimes, the Message *Is* the Message

What if some reborn shaman enters the world, begins to relate that portion of the truth, and people don't or can't understand?

> There's no guarantee that anyone is going to **believe** the shaman, even if the sha-

man speaks up: look at Cassandra, cursed
by Apollo to tell the truth, and when she
did, no one would believe her. Imagine how
maddening that would be. Well, speaking
the truth of our impossible genders is just
like that.

I think it's up to the shaman to figure out a way to make that truth understandable in this world. I think it's *how you tell the truth* as much as what you're saying: that's Marshall McLuhan's medium as message as massage, form being every bit as important as content. Culture itself is an acceptable performance of a truth, or a truth with an easy learning curve—people understand the culture. The shaman needs to communicate/perform that truth in such a way that the culture can hear it.

Science is a way of talking about the
universe in words that bind it to a com-
mon reality. Magic is a method of talking
to the universe in words that it cannot
ignore. The two are rarely compatible.

—Neil Gaiman,
The Invisible Labyrinth, 1993

The truth of the shaman is the performance of the shaman, a performance that can't be ignored. With this performance, the shaman performs (creates) the culture. The essential tool of the shaman is paradox: a presence that is absent or, equally, an absence that is present.

The phenomenon of transsexualism is
both a confirmation of the construct-
edness of gender and a secondary re-
course to essentialism—or, to put it a

slightly different way, transsexualism
demonstrates that essentialism is a cul-
tural construction.
   —*Marjorie Garber,* Vested Interests: Cross-
         Dressing and Cultural Anxiety, *1992*

Finally, You Kiss It Better

The value of the paradox is its ability to ease the suffering of others by entangling two seemingly opposing forces or ideas—to bind two edges of a torn and bleeding wound. This kind of healing is traditional in any shamanic culture. Like good art and good sex, good healing can be transformational, blurring the lines between life and death. The healing acts of a Gender Transcender, or shaman, might begin with the dissolving of gender and gender boundaries. But gender, while a basic building block to our culture, is very likely not the final challenge for anyone who truly wants to fix the mess we've gotten ourselves into.

» *Basic health and well-being mean*
   the panoramic perception of all lev-
   els of being.
» *Healing means healing culture first,*
   then people, and finally sickness.
» *Holiness means feeling many—all—*
   spheres of existence within oneself.
      —*Holger Kalweit,* Shamans, Healers, and
                     Medicine Men, *1992*

The Catch, and How to Avoid It

There's a trap for shamans: there's a cultural tendency to deify the shaman as role model, pop icon, guru, or literally goddess or god. Take, for example, the deification of the ambiguously gendered Marlene Dietrich or Michael Jackson. Deification fixes the shaman into a particular role or identity, with no room to move around, no room to grow. Like the fool, the shaman can't be bound up in any single identity; the shaman can't take sides or be part of any identity politics. The shaman needs to seek broader and broader groups of people to serve. By staying in a fixed time and place, the shaman's message will be repeated over and over again only to those who've already heard it, and then the madness sets in. The shaman needs to remain outside any binary, in some third space, a space that constantly shifts and changes.

The "third" is that which questions binary thinking and introduces crisis. . . . [T]he "third" is a mode of articulation, a way of describing a space of possibility. Three puts in question the idea of one: of identity, self-sufficiency, self-knowledge.

   —Marjorie Garber, Vested Interests: Cross-
         Dressing and Cultural Anxiety, 1992

The concept of the "third" is the concept of the outlaw, who understands the universal constancy of change, outside any given dichotomy. I think anyone who regularly walks along a forbidden boundary or border (queer/straight, sober/drunk, female/male, black/white, etc.) has the potential to attain some degree of spiritual awareness. The task for those who take that road is, usually, to point a way out of struggle and suffering for as many people as possible, and that begins with raising questions and implicating people. We raise different questions depending on where we live. For example, I live at the fun-filled intersection of art, politics, class, and the academy. But because I'm not really a member of any of these groups, I raise questions like:

Economics—

» If wealth and power are important, and if in this world wealth and power belong to men, then why did I cease being a man and give up that wealth and power?

» What is the value of wealth and power?

Sexuality—

» If men are supposed to love women and women are supposed to love men, then what am I if I love women?

» And what are you if you are attracted to me?

» What are we if we become lovers, you and I?

» What is the nature of your desire?

Rather than wallow in self-pity or boil in some cauldron of rage and injustice, I think it's time for trans people—whether binary or nonbinary identified—to come together under our own banner: a banner that would include anyone who cares to own their own gender ambiguities, a banner that includes trans of all sexualities, races and ethnicities, religions, ages, classes, and states of body, a banner of the Third.

I think it's time for us to use our status as Third to bring some harmony into the world. Like other border outlaws, trans people are here to open some doorway that's been closed off for a long, long time. We're gatekeepers, nothing more.

The Tao gives birth to One.
One gives birth to Two.

Two gives birth to Three.
Three gives birth to all things.
          —*Lao-Tzu,* Tao Te Ching, *1988*

Before going through with my surgery, before creating myself in Third, I asked questions, as many as possible, as many as I could think of. And I wrote down all the questions that people asked me. Before creating a Third Space, it might be a good idea to make sure all the questions that need asking actually get asked, as many as possible.

a gender interrogatory

Beyond questions like "Can you orgasm with that vagina?"
there are questions that can actually make it easier to live a
life in harmony with this world, out of the closet, and into the
sunshine. These are some of the questions I could think up. I
welcome any other questions like these: you can write me care
of my publisher, or tweet me at @katebornstein. If I'm still
alive, I'll try my best to get back to you.

Warrant Officer Al Bornstein, first mate aboard the
seagoing yacht Apollo, at the time the flagship of the Church
of Scientology.

THE FIRST QUESTION

or, They Have Those Funny, Staring Eyes

The first question needs a lot of space all to itself. The first question is the one that seems to get asked the least frequently: namely, why in the world are we hanging on to gender, and to our gender systems?

> I heard once that "Why?" is not a spiritual question. Perhaps not. But it **is** a political question, and politics seems to be as good a step as any on the road to spirituality.

Given any binary, it's *fun* to look for some hidden third, and the reason why the third was hidden says a lot about a culture. The choice between two of *anything* is not a choice at all but rather the opportunity to subscribe to the value system that holds the two presented choices as mutually exclusive alternatives. Once we choose one or the other, we've given up our imagination in favor of buying into the system that perpetuates that binary. When, for example, I lived my life saying I was a man or a woman, I was tacitly supporting all the rules of the gender system that defines those two identities. I supported those rules in order to belong, or rather to not be an outsider, a non-belonger.

Imagine belonging to gender in the same way that we belong to:

Google+, YouTube, Facebook, etc.

The Kiwanis

The Democratic Party

A health club

A jury

A credit union

A frequent-flier program

The military

A corporation

A singles club

A 12-step program

The gender system that most people practice in the Eurocentric culture of the first quarter of the twenty-first century is the **real** Boys Club and Girls Club!

I began to analyze gender dynamics in terms of group dynamics. One fascinating point stood out as relevant to both gender and group dynamics, providing a link between the two: compliance within a group is set by the naming of good and bad behavior; the former is laudable, the latter is punishable. *Either/or* is used as a control mechanism, as in, "Either you live up to our high standards here in the club, or your membership will be revoked."

"Ladies" are the kind of people who won't let my girlfriend use the public ladies' room, thinking she's not a woman. Oh, but they're not going to let her use the men's room either—they're not going to let her be a man either. If she's not a man, and she's not a woman, then what is she? Once I asked my mother

what fire was: a solid, liquid, or gas?
And she said it wasn't any one of those
things—it was something that happened
to things: a force of nature, she called it.

Maybe that's what she is: a force of
nature. For sure she is something that
happened to me.

—Holly Hughes, "Clit Notes," 1993

It's just like . . . Family, yeah . . . Family, that's it!

What if the binary gender system *really was a group*, just like the
Tea Party, or your grandparents' weekly bridge club? And if its
members were blindly following rules that they neither question
nor were even capable of challenging, then the group becomes
more like a cult. There are patterns, both structural and behavioral, common to cults. For a long time, I was a member of Scientology, so perhaps I'm sensitive to recognizing those patterns,
even in groups not traditionally defined as cults.

The more I thought about it, the more I loved the idea of
looking at gender as a cult, so I put it to a few tests. For example:
cults, like most groups, need to defend their boundaries, their
borders, and gender, as a cult, would need to do the same.

> It was really difficult to leave the group
> of . . . what should we call it? The gen-
> dered? Sure. It was really difficult to leave
> that group when I embraced my nonbinary
> gender identity. I cannot think of many
> cisgender people who encouraged me or
> even wished me well. In the same way that
> some cults keep their followers under lock
> and key, the gendered keep their number

under tight control and surveillance. To lose a member (did I say that?) would be unthinkable.

Compliance with a group often means demonstrating one's allegiance through round-the-clock participation in the forwarding of the group's goals. Some marginalized communities demand this in the name of activism. In a cult, this day-and-night participation is often a requirement for continued membership. Similarly, within the cult of gender, members are required to weave the continual maintenance of the cult into their daily lives. Questions can go a long way toward breaking cult patterns.

> » Do you ever go to sleep at night wondering what gender you are?
> » Have you ever seriously questioned which bathroom to use—men's or women's . . . or whether you need a third bathroom?
> » Do you buy your clothes mostly from some gender-specific store or department of a store?
> » Do you belong to or support some men-only or women-only club?
> » Do you think I'm a former man, and that I'm now a woman?
> » Do you think I'm still a man?
> » Have you examined your own gender and decided beyond a shadow of a doubt, based on examination, that you really are that one gender?
> » Do you express your gender naturally, or has it taken some practice on your part?

In some cults, demonstrating allegiance frequently means attacking the enemies of the cult.

> [The] dissident [in any group] is criticized as disloyal, lacking commitment, interfering with the important work of the group.
>
> —Arthur J. Deikman,
> The Wrong Way Home: Uncovering
> Patterns of Cult Behavior in
> American Society, 1990

And so we have a good excuse for violence in the name of heteronormativity and cisnormativity. The grounds for homophobia has less to do, I think, with sexual orientation than it does with gender expression. When a gay man is bashed on the street, it's unlikely that the bashers are thinking of the gay man butt-fucking anyone or in fact being butt-fucked. It has little to do with imagining that man sucking cock. It has a lot to do with seeing that man violate the rules of gender in this culture. The first commandment in this culture for men is "Thou shalt be neither a woman, nor womanly." And the corresponding commandment for a woman in this culture is "Thou shalt be neither a man, nor manly."

> » Do you think you have it in you to be a man?
> » Do you think you have it in you to be a woman?
> » Have you ever thought what it might be like to be neither for a day? An hour? One whole minute?

The most obviously violent structure within the cult of gender is sexism, misogyny. Misogyny is necessary to maintain the cult of gender, the struggle to be one or the other. The dynamic is similar to the power structure of a nation needing an enemy, be it Hitler, an evil empire, or a Hitler-like madman.

> Growing up, the one thing that was consistent in my family, and in the families of all my friends, was an interesting form of misogyny. It was the one area in which I was consistently told **NO**. No, you cannot behave like, look like, or be a girl. An excellent analysis of misogyny leveled at trans people may be found in **Whipping Girl**, by Julia Serano.

Gender as a System of Oppression

A particularly insidious aspect of gender—our gender system here in the West, and perhaps for the planet as a whole—is that it is an oppressive class system made all the more dangerous by the belief that it is an entirely natural state of affairs. In this sense, gender is no different a form of class oppression than the caste system in India or apartheid in South Africa. Those systems have long been held to be "natural," and the way of the world in their respective cultures, based as they are on the concept of the possibility of a pure identity.

Purity of identity is essential to identity politics, wherein membership is only permitted after proof of a pure identity, devoid of entanglement with any other identity. That holds true whether we're talking left-wing or right-wing politics. What, after all, are the differences between demanding racial purity, ethnic purity, ideological, moral, or religious purity, and, in the case of gender, gender purity? What is purity anyway? Who gets to decide? Members of the club assume *they're* pure, and it's only us outsiders who wonder what we have to do in order to be allowed in.

In going from male to female, I discovered that men don't seem to think about gender in the same way women do. The preferred gender in our patriarchal society is male, and so males mostly take gender for granted, most men do not try to analyze what it means to be male. Even the men's movement seems more predicated on a desire to not be drawn into some web of femininity, rather than a desire to **question** the construct of male identity. Women, on the other hand, have been taught that they're the "second sex," the distaff gender, so their lives are an almost daily struggle with the concept of gender. The trap for women is the system itself: it's not men who are the foe so much as it is the binary gender system that keeps men in place as more privileged.

Struggle and privilege, insiders and outsiders—these are some fairly common phenomena—but common to what? Cults? Well, yes, but as cute as the analogy may be, and as wickedly accurate as some of the points may be, gender as cult is not a one-to-one correspondence. Then it hit me that gender struggles have historically failed to reach their goals, whereas class conflicts have historically had some degree of success.

The progress of women's rights in our culture, unlike other types of "progress," has always been strangely reversible.

—*Ann Douglas,* The Feminization of
American Culture, *1977*

It's time to call the persistent clash of genders what it really is: a class conflict within a dangerously invisible and pervasive cult-like class system. Gender is indeed a group, a club, a faith—but it operates as a class system, pervasively, throughout the culture.

> The continued oppression of women proves only that in any binary there's going to be one up and one down. The fight for gender justice must include the fight to dismantle the binary.

I got real curious about my position as former-man and not-quite-woman. Where did that place me in the gender/class struggle that was daily spinning itself out in our culture?

Paul Fussell, in his book *Class,* outlines nine different classes in the United States. He then devotes his final chapter to something he calls an "X" class: people who manage to live outside the class system. Try substituting the word "gender" for the word "class" in the following paragraph.

> "X" people are better conceived as belonging to a category than a class because you are not born an X person, as you are born and reared a prole or a middle. You become an X person, or, to put it more bluntly, you earn X-personhood by a strenuous effort of discovery in which curiosity and originality are indispensable. And in discovering that you can become an X person you find the only escape from class. Entering category X often requires flight from parents and forebears. . . . X people can be described as "self-cultivated."
>
> —Paul Fussell, Class, 1984

Gender, Class, and Power

In the either/or gender class system that we call male and female, the structure of one up, one down fulfills the requisite for a perpetual power imbalance. It became clear that the reason the binary gender system continues to exist, and is actively and tenaciously held in place, is that the binary gender system is primarily a venue for the playing out of a power game. It's an arena in which roughly half the people in the world can have power over the other half.

Without the structure of the binary gender system, the power dynamic between men and women shatters. People would not have gender to use as a hierarchical framework, and nearly half the members of the binary gender system would probably be at quite a loss. They believe (foolishly, I think) that the power they have and exert over others is a good thing, and they want to hang on to it; they're terrified of losing this stuff. What I'm talking about is what's been called "male privilege." And I think this is the crux of the gender issue; this is what's holding gender in place: people who have and exert male privilege just don't want to give it up. I think that male privilege is the glue that holds the system together.

> People ask me what it was like to have had that kind of privilege, what it was like to lose it, why in the world I gave it up. To have it was like taking drugs; to get rid of it was like kicking a habit. I gave it up because it was destroying me and the people I loved.

Exerting "male privilege" is acting on the assumption that one has the right to occupy any space or person by whatever means, with or without permission. It's a sense of entitlement that's unique to those who have been raised male in most cultures—it's notably absent in most girls and women. Male privilege is not something that's given to men in this culture; it's something that men take. It's not that women don't have the ability to have and wield this privilege; some do. It's that in most cases, this privilege is withheld from them culturally and emotionally. Male privilege is woven into all levels of the culture, from unearned higher wages to more opportunities in the workplace, from higher quality, less-expensive clothing to better bathroom facilities. Male privilege extends into sexual harassment, rape, and war. Combine male privilege with capitalism (which rewards greed and acquisition) and the mass media (which, owned by capitalists, highlights only the rewards of acquisition and makes invisible its penalties), and you have a juggernaut that needs stopping by any means. Male privilege is not the exclusive province of men; there are some few women who have a degree of this horrifying personality trait. The wielding of male privilege is, in a word, violence.

> An interesting way to negotiate a truce in the "war between the sexes" in the United States would be to mandate not an increase in wages for women but rather a **decrease** in wages for **men** to the level of any woman holding a similar position. Use the money thus saved to repay a deficit. Or fund the arts. Or help out homeless queer youth. I wonder how far that would fly in a male-dominated legislature?

Whatever the idea might be that hopes to end the suffering of women on this planet, it's going to require men giving up privilege, and then all of us giving up this rigid binary gender system. Un-privileging is a necessary prior condition for the deconstruction of the gender system.

More on Male Privilege

To this day, I'm involved in a delightful, decades-long correspondence with Caitlin Sullivan, radical butch dyke and freelance editor. She asks me challenging questions, which turn me on as much as any flirtation.

Re the male privilege thing. Why are the male-to-females so reluctant to admit this? Do they want to pretend they were never male? By the same token, could you elaborate on what it felt like to lose that privilege? You've described having it—were you aware at the time? What were the ways you noticed you didn't have it anymore? And, what have you retained as a result of having had it? Confidence springs to mind, is that true?

—Caitlin Sullivan, in correspondence
with the author, 1993

I'm not sure I'm any more or less confident as a result of having lived a life with male privilege, Caitlin. Maybe it's more that I know how to act confident even when I'm not.

I don't know why some male-to-females you met were reluctant to admit having had (or having) male privilege. For me, I just wasn't aware of any general impunity when I had it. I can understand men looking baffled when women accuse them of exercising male privilege; it's like many white people who look blank when confronted with their racism. It's also like cisgender people who look blank when confronted with their transphobia (defined as fear and mistreatment of people who are differently gendered).

I didn't "lose" my male privilege so much as I made a conscious decision to get rid of it, and I didn't get rid of it all at once; it's an attitude that is insidiously pervasive. At this writing, some thirty years after my transition out of male, the point where my vestigial privilege is most likely to surface is when I'm driving: I can be quite a terror. Sigh.

It took my becoming a woman to discover my "male

behavior"—that is, exhibiting male privilege. When I was first coming out as trans, I used to hang out mostly with women. Any act of mine that was learned male behavior stuck out like a sore thumb. Things like leaping up and taking charge, even when it wasn't called for; things like wielding language like a sledge-hammer; or assuming that everyone owed me special consideration for my journey through a gender change—I still shudder at my arrogance. Some might say none of that's male. Well, I learned it when I was a guy, and I was the only one exhibiting that behavior when I was in the company of women, so if it's not exclusively male, it's real close. My friend Michelle Moran laughs and says she can spot the male sense of entitlement in trans women who insist on acceptance as women. "They wanna be women," she jokes, "let 'em start with a good dose of humility."

I noticed I didn't have much remaining male privilege by the slow dawning of peacefulness in my life. That may sound new-agey, but the fact is I'm nowhere near as territorial and possessive as I used to be. I'm not as frantic to get or hold on to something as I once was. I still want things. I still go after things. But I use force infrequently now. For me, that's a perk of having gotten rid of male privilege. The shortcomings are obvious: lower pay, less security, more fear on the streets, less opportunity in the job market. All those drawbacks made me look at the value of what I'd lost. Do I really want to take part in a culture that places a higher value on greed and acquisition than on peace and shared growth?

One of the things that makes me, and others like me, dangerous is that we do speak up. We break the silence imposed on our people. And what we talk about is the very real oppression of women. In my case, I'm not theorizing about it like a man would . . . I have consciously given up and set aside my male privilege and I am now experiencing life as very different and non-privileged. And there are plenty of people who wouldn't want me to talk about this. I break this silence, and the silence is what keeps any binary, and the oppression done in its name, in place.

This book, and the many other words, acts, art, video, and politics of other gender activists attest that it's a time of cultural readiness for these theories—these ambiguities. We might actually be making more progress in the area of gender than we're aware of: more and more people are asking questions, and that's a good sign. We just haven't been measuring that progress by a yardstick that everyone can agree on. We haven't dared to name a goal: probably something like "a society free from the constraints of nonconsensual gender."

I love the idea of men voluntarily giving up their male privilege—it would be great to figure out some means of measuring that stuff dropping by the wayside, and the positive effect that has on the culture.

King Lear, in the 1969 Brown University production of Shakespeare's King Lear, directed by James O. Barnhill. I'd like to do more Shakespeare—the women, or maybe the men.

12

THE OTHER QUESTIONS

Once I have restored Hollywood to its ancient glory (and myself to what I was!), I shall very simply restructure the human race. This will entail the reduction of world population through a complete change in man's sexual image.

—Gore Vidal, Myron, 1974

1. Where does gender come from? Where does it keep coming from?

Is it really "natural"? What has gender got to do with penises, vaginas, chromosomes, or clothing? With hormones, lipstick, breasts, baldness, or beards?

Gender could be seen as a class system. By having gender around, there are these two classes—male and female. As in any binary, one side will always have more power than the other. One will always seek dominance over the other. The value of a two-gender system is nothing more than the value of keeping the power imbalance, and all that depends on that, intact.

2. Can there be an equality between genders?

Or is "equality of the genders" oxymoronic, making any fight for the equality of the genders self-defeating? Gender implies class, and class presupposes inequality. Fight rather to defuse and deconstruct the enforcement of binary gender—it would get to the same place much faster.

But rather than look at some underlying reason for inequality, most people keep going on about the differences between the (two only) genders. The differences are only what we decide they are. And when some set of differences changes a little with time and culture, we call those changes making progress in the area of gender, but gender is still there.

> » I'm tall, and I'm a big-boned gal. When I began living as a woman, men started opening doors for me, offering to carry packages, letting me go first down passageways. I was really puzzled. On the one hand, I was glad to be perceived as a woman; on the other hand, I didn't appreciate being treated like a child.

> » But living on the flip side of gendered etiquette was only the beginning. I'd been in quite a few sales jobs—I knew how to sell . . . as a man. As a woman, the clients didn't want to hear my "expert opinion." As a woman, the clients wanted to hear me say, "Well, you know better than me, Mr. Jones—what do **you** think?"

> » As a man, I had access to work, and when I was out of work, I had very free access to job interviews. As a woman, **for the first time in my life**, I was told to not bother coming in for an interview.

> » The differences in the way men and women are treated are real. And the fact is this difference in treatment has no basis in the differences between men and women. I was the same person, and I was treated entirely differently. I got

real interested in feminist theory—real
fast.

There are differences enforced by the culture, and these need to be dealt with, but these differences are not intrinsic to the genders. By focusing on so-called inherent differences between men and women, we ignore and deny the existence of the gender system itself, and so we in fact hold it in place. But it's the enforced gender system itself, the idea of "natural gender," that needs to be done away with—or at least disempowered. The differences will then fall aside of their own accord.

I can see no other ethical basis for a reconciliation [between men and women] than the feminist principle—so often repeated—that women are also persons, with the same needs for respect, for satisfying work, for love and pleasure— as men.

—*Barbara Ehrenreich*, The Hearts of Men:
American Dreams and the Flight from
Commitment, 1984

3. Just how integral is gender to the culture?
Well, it's a patriarchal culture, and gender seems to be basic to the patriarchy. After all, men couldn't have male privilege if there were no males. And women couldn't be oppressed if there was no such thing as "women." Doing away with enforced binary gender is key to doing away with the patriarchy, as well as ending the many injustices perpetrated in the name of gender inequity. There is no gender inequity that doesn't first assume there is gender—and only two genders at that. Gender inequities include sexism, homophobia, transphobia, and misogyny.

The struggle for women's rights (and, to a lesser extent, men's rights) is a vital stopgap measure until we do away with the system whose very nature maintains the imbalance and prohibits any harmony.

4. Is androgyny desirable or attainable?

Androgyny assumes that there's male stuff on one side of a spectrum and female stuff on another side of that spectrum. And somewhere in the middle of this straight line there's an ideal blend of "male" and "female." That's much better than saying either/or. However, by saying there's a "middle," androgyny really keeps the opposites in place. By saying that we have a "male side" and a "female side," we blind ourselves to all the beautiful shades of identity of which we are each capable. Androgyny could be seen as a trap of the binary gender system, as it further establishes the idea of two-and-only-two genders.

Instead of imagining gender as opposite poles of a two-dimensional line, it would be interesting to twirl that line in space, and then spin it through several more dimensions. In this way, many more possibilities of gender identity may be explored.

> Exercise: Make a list of all the genders you observe in a week.
> Exercise: Make a list of all the genders you've been in a week.
> Exercise: Make a list of all the genders you can imagine in a week.

5. What is the source of gender's power?

Many cultures believe that names have power, and that by hiding one's name, one cannot be harmed. Calling someone or something by its real name strips it of its power.

Names in general are very powerful, and most philosophies acknowledge that. The Old Testament says that the first act of humankind was to name things on the planet. The suit of swords in the tarot deck is the suit of naming, separating things out. (To this day, a sword is used in the naming ceremonies of English royalty.) But the suit of swords (which became spades in our modern decks) is viewed as the suit of ruin, despair, and bad luck—which is what you get, apparently, when you mess around with separating things out and naming them.

If you must name something, please look for the oppression and name it—give it some trouble; its name may well be gender. Please—don't call it "biological sex" or "social gender." Don't call it "sex" at all—sex is fucking; gender is everything else. Gender hides behind a great number of false names, and these names are all "types" of gender. But types of gender don't reveal anything about gender. Types of gender only reveal the paranoias of the societies that construct the types. Gender *becomes* typed in an attempt to hold together the boundaries of a given group. We can start doing away with gender by calling it gender.

6. How do people become gendered?
It depends on where you're sitting, but the system doesn't let you sit apart from gender for very long. The gender system of this culture fosters cultlike behavior. After all, membership in a gender is not based on informed consent. There is no possibility of abandoning membership without censure, ridicule, and danger. Members have no sense of humor regarding the cult of gender. Any humor that does exist about gender is based on the ridicule of its transgressors and nonmembers. Gender could use a good

belly laugh at its own expense, but cults rarely get to laugh at themselves.

7. How does gender relate to identity?

Most of us assume that there *is* gender; that there are only two categories of gender, and that we are (i.e., occupy the identity of) one or the other. We have a lot invested in this belief—it's very difficult to imagine ourselves genderless. It's difficult to the degree that our identities are wrapped up in our (completely arbitrary) gender assignments. We need to differentiate between *having* an identity and *being* an identity.

It's a fairly well-accepted principle that we seem to get into trouble when we define ourselves by things outside of ourselves. There are growing numbers of support groups dedicated to extricating their members from identity entanglements with one addiction or another—and these addictions are to things outside ourselves. There's trouble in defining ourselves by the food we eat, the drugs we take, or the kind of entertainment we like to indulge in. There's also trouble in defining ourselves by our jobs, our relationships, our income level, our belongings, our age, our sexual orientation, our class, our politics, or our geography. All these things are transient, and when these things change—and change they do—we have identity crises.

> I mapped out the recurring pattern of the several identity crises I've experienced in my life: first I question an identity that I have, then I see all its bad qualities, and eventually I lose it or give it up. Then I get what seems to be a new, more pure, more unshakable identity—maybe I call it my authentic self—and I go through learning the ropes about what it means to be that new identity. Then, once I'm comfortable

in the new identity, I question that, and the identity crisis starts all over again. It's what I did with gender; it's what I'm still doing with gender.

It's the grasping for gender—any gender—that's always been a cause of my suffering. How about you? Are you grasping for any particular aspect of gender? What might it feel like to stop grasping?

An identity crisis can occur around gender identity, except we usually don't notice it because we're so convinced that gender itself is immutable and thereby immune to crisis. By defining ourselves as genderless, however, there's one less distraction to the development of our own integrity. Please, assume no gender.

The "third" is that which questions binary thinking and introduces crisis.
—Marjorie Garber, Vested Interests: Cross-Dressing and Cultural Anxiety, *1992*

8. What's the difference between transsexual and transgender?

Both words are used to define ourselves as men and women who have transitioned from another gender. *Transsexual* is most generally used by people who define their transition in medical terms of surgery and hormones. People who claim a transgender identity may or may not opt for surgery and/or hormones as a part of their transition.

Nearly everyone has some sort of bone to pick with their own gender status, be it gender role, gender assignment, or gender identity. And when this dissatisfaction can no longer be glossed over with good manners, or cured by purchasing enough gender-specific products or services—and when this dissatisfaction cannot be silenced by the authority of the state, the medical profession, the church, or one's own peers—then the dissatisfaction is called transgender, or transsexual, or gender dysphoria. We're most of us—whether trans or not—dissatisfied. Some of us have less tolerance for the dissatisfaction, that's all. I accept the label "transsexual" as meaning only that I was dissatisfied with my given gender, and I acted to change it. I am transsexual by choice, not by pathology.

> I'm called "gender dysphoric." That means I have a sickness: a limited understanding of gender. I don't think it's that. I like to look at it that I **was** gender dysphoric for my whole life before, and for some time after my gender change—bullied into blindly buying into the gender system. As soon as I came to some understanding about the constructed nature of gender, and my relationship to that system, I ceased being gender dysphoric. Nowadays, I'm positively gender euphoric.

People think they have to hate their genitals in order to be transgender. Well, some trans men and women do hate their genitals, and they act to change them. Some don't. But none of us hates any part of our bodies we weren't *taught* to hate. We're taught to hate parts of our bodies that aren't "natural"—like a penis on a woman, or a vagina on a man—and it seems that the arbiters of nature are the doctors.

The belief that gender is based on genitals is a medicalized belief. The term *transsexual* was invented by a doctor. The system of legalized gender transition by means of hormones and surgery is perpetuated by doctors. But the demedicalization of transgender is a dilemma. There are always going to be folks in need of genital surgery. Due to financial requirements, the fulfillment of a surgical dream is subject to cultural and class constraints; cosmetic and genital conversion surgery is available primarily to the middle and upper classes. So, transsexuals are heavily invested in maintaining their status as "diseased" people, because any demedicalization of transsexuality could further limit surgery in this culture, as it would remove the label of "illness" and so prohibit insurance companies from footing the bill.

> I had my genital surgery partially as a result of cultural pressure: I couldn't be a "real woman" as long as I had a penis. Knowing what I know now, I'm still glad I had my genital surgery, and I'd do it again, just for the comfort I now feel with a constructed vagina. I **like** that thang!

Loren Cameron puts forward the theory that there is a continuum of managing one's gender. For some people, comfort is only achieved through genital surgery; for others, no genital modification is felt to be necessary; and for still others, an occasional evening of dress-up suffices just fine. Each of us needs to name and attain our own point of comfort. Insurance-based coverage for genital surgery should, I believe, be made available for those who can't afford it, and for whom the comfort point would require that surgery.

To some transsexuals, the state of transsexuality itself is seen as transitory—a cocoon. In goes one gender, out comes the other. So there's a pre-transition and post-transition trans person. Through its insistence and fierce maintenance of the man / woman dichotomy, the culture puts the pre-transition person in the position of needing to say a permanent good-bye to one gender, and then and only then saying hello to another. While that good-bye/hello is certainly an option, this culture is making it the *only* option. A viable solution to such a "choice" is to disentangle yourself long enough from the culture or individual presenting the two alternatives that you can explore some other options. One option to keep in mind is that transition is possible without any medical intervention whatsoever.

Anne Bolin describes gender transition in terms of an anthropological model: the individual withdraws from the culture, its rules and its company, in order to effect the loss of one identity and the taking-on of another. That new identity firmly in place, the post-transition individual then reenters the culture. The process is nearly identical to the breakup of a relationship: we leave behind one gender/partner in order to engage with another.

Negative definitions of partner and relationship precede and accompany the leavetaking because the loss must be turned into an acceptable loss. We justify our failure to ourselves by dwelling on the negative aspects of what we are leaving behind.

—*Diane Vaughan,* Uncoupling: How
Relationships Come Apart, *1987*

It's the old story of devaluing the outsider, only in this case, the outsider is the gender one is taking leave of. By devaluing the gender left behind, the transsexual perpetuates the "war" between the genders.

Trans folks who identify as nonbinary, genderqueer, agender, gender nonconforming, gender fluid, and the like assess their journey not as either/or but rather as an integration, a whole. In bypassing the either/or construct, they bypass defining components of transsexual and now transgender identities. These new trans people are slipping out from under the control of the culture. And a new subculture is being born, to join the binary subcultures of transsexuals and transgenders as members of a larger, more inclusive subculture: trans.

So, who is trans? Anyone who admits it—admitting is difficult, because after you admit it you then have to own it.

Practically speaking, trans is anyone whose personal management of gender identity and/or gender expression consumes a great deal of their day-to-day life.

All trans activism—binary and nonbinary alike—raises questions about gender, and that makes me very happy.

All trans people everywhere share the challenge of living as a marginalized and oppressed person, to one degree or another. That's just the way it is. In some cultures, we are literally stoned to death for owning and expressing our authentic selves. At best, we might get laughed at, joked about, or misgendered a couple of times a week. The way trans people respond to oppression varies, but almost always includes both some degree of assimilation and some degree of thumbing our nose at the culture that would rather see us dead.

9. How does gender relate to power?

Power seems basic to gender, and gets played out *through* gender, usually without the permission or even the understanding of the people involved in the playing.

*To change [gender] is to slide along a
power differential. To change power is
to change [gender].*
  —Marjorie Garber, Vested Interests: Cross-
          Dressing and Cultural Anxiety, 1992

The current gender system relies heavily on everyone's agreement that it's inflexible. Key to the doing away with gender is the
ability to freely move into and out of existing genders and gender
roles. Like butch and femme. Like top and bottom. And, eventually, like man and woman. BDSM is a consensual way to play with
power and gender through sex.

BDSM includes all forms of consensual bondage and disci-
pline, dominance and submission, and sadism and masochism.
There are several ways to look at BDSM, depending on degrees
of sex/gender positivity and sex/gender negativity. The conservative or puritanical wing of the sexuality and gender debates
views BDSM as nonconsensual violence, rape, and other forms of
unspeakable cruelty and oppression. Most practitioners—and I'm
one—see BDSM as both loving and consensual. One (or more)
person is top, or dominant; one (or more) person is bottom, or
submissive. In many cases, BDSM players negotiate their needs,
their wants, their fantasies, and their restrictions (medical, emotional, psychological, etc.) prior to any actual playing.

Playing is one term commonly used to describe BDSM sexual
activities. Those who are playing have agreed upon their roles,
and the boundaries within which they will play. In most scenar-
ios, there are ways to end the play or exit the scene safely and
quickly if it's becoming too much for one or more of the players. Discussions abound within the BDSM communities about
who holds the power: the top or the bottom. Most players agree
that power is *shared,* with the top in control but only within the
bounds agreed upon and often requested by the bottom. Some
say there's a sublime moment when top and bottom together and
at once have all the power and none of the power.

BDSM play can accommodate any combination of sex, power, and gender play. When the play reaches the point of almost purely dealing with power, then many BDSMers agree that gender has in fact been done away with.

> This could possibly contribute to the current taboos placed on BDSM by leaders of some branches of feminism, as well as by the more vocally conservative patriarchy: they're both heavily invested in maintaining their genders and the binary system that defines their own boundaries, self-definitions, and ideologies.

In the late 1980s, I was a member of the Outcasts, a San Francisco–based women's S/M organization.

> S/M was more or less the umbrella term for all BDSM play back then, and sadomasochism has always been my BDSM personal yum—I'm a longtime masochist, and submissive. And in the first edition of this book, I wrote the following section from that point of view. But really, everything that follows is applicable to most any form of BDSM. Okay, here we go …

The Outcasts defined three keys to sadomasochistic play: S/M must be safe, sane, and consensual—by playing this way, S/M uncovers the hidden power games of the culture. Safe, sane, and consensual sadomasochism necessitates *talking* about these games. On a day-to-day basis, we may get caught up in some cultural power games without wanting to get so entangled. In S/M, we *play* at these power games because the playing is fun. Similarly, we can play at gender precisely because it is fun.

I spoke once at an Outcasts meeting about gender play and S/M play:

> I think gender can take a lesson from S/M: gender needs to be safe, sane, and consensual.
>
> Gender is not safe.
> If I change my gender, I'm at risk of homicide, suicide, or a life devoid of half my possibilities.
> If I'm born with a body that gives mixed gender signals, I'm at risk of being butchered—fixed, mutilated. Gender is not safe.
>
> And gender is not sane.
> It's not sane to call a rainbow black and white.
> It's not sane to demand we fit into one or the other only.
> It's not sane that we classify people in order to oppress them as women or to glorify them as men.
> Gender is not sane.
>
> And gender is not consensual.
> We're born: a doctor assigns us a gender. It's documented by the state, enforced by the legal profession, sanctified by the church, and it's bought and sold in the media. We have no say in our gender—we're not allowed to question it, play with it, work it out with our friends, lovers, or family.
> Gender is not consensual.

Safe gender is being who and what we want to be when we want to be that, and expressing ourselves with no threat of censure or violence. Safe gender is going as far in any direction as we wish, with no threat to our health, or to anyone else's.

Safe gender is not being pressured into passing, not having to lie, not having to hide.

Sane gender is asking questions about gender—talking to people who do gender, and opening up about our gender histories and our gender desires.

Sane gender is probably very, very funny.

Consensual gender is respecting one anothers' definitions of gender—whether binary or nonbinary—and respecting the wishes of some to be alone, and respecting the intentions of others to be inclusive in their own time.

Consensual gender is nonviolent in that it doesn't force its way in on anyone.

Consensual gender opens its arms and welcomes all people as gender outcasts—whoever is willing to admit to it.

Gender has a lot to learn from S/M.

And we who know S/M are a lot further along the road to safe, sane, consensual gender play than we may realize. We just need to apply the basics.

If living gender-free can shine a light on personal identity, then living with S/M can illuminate interpersonal dynamics. S/M as a sexual preference is an alternative to the hetero/homo dichotomy served up in this culture.

Sadomasochism intersects gender at the point of performance. We perform our identities, which include gender, and we perform our relationships, which include sex. Transgender is simply an identity more consciously performed on the infrequently used playing field of gender. S/M is simply a relationship more consciously performed within the forbidden arena of power.

S/M partners may also play at what the culture often refuses to acknowledge about itself—owning or belonging to one another. This game highlights factors basic to power: the need to belong, and its two corollaries, the need to own and the need to exclude. We rarely think about the concept of belonging to something as "being owned" by something, but that's what it means. This culture teaches us to belong to one gender or another, in the same way that we're taught we need to *own* a home, *belong* to a nuclear family, *have* a profession, *occupy* a geographical location, and let's not forget we need a place to call our *own*.

Our culture also tells us that we are what we belong to. To give up membership is to give up identity, and while that's not ultimately harmful, it is frightening. In the same way we unlearn other outmoded and/or harmful cultural imperatives, we need to unlearn gender. In the same way we need to break free of systems that enslave us, we need to break free of gender. The fear and hatred of gender outlaws and S/M players is the fear and hatred of those who do not belong, who are nonconsensually or unconsciously owned lock, stock, and barrel by the binary gender system and those who support, maintain, and enforce it.

10. Why is there so much emphasis on passing?
Passing is a form of pretending, which can be fun. In gender, passing is defined as the act of appearing in the world as a gender to which one does not belong, or as a gender to which one did not

formerly belong. Much passing is undertaken in response to the cultural imperative to be one gender or the other. In this case, passing becomes the outward manifestation of shame and capitulation. Passing becomes silence. Passing becomes invisibility. Passing becomes lies. Passing becomes self-denial.

A more universal and less depressing definition of passing would be the act of appearing in the gender of one's choice. Everyone is passing; some have an easier job of it than others.

> I identify as nonbinary trans. My most joyful gender expression is as female. I'm not genderqueer—I don't aim to mix up my gender expression. As out of the closet as I am on a very broad public level, I still make every effort to be pretty according to my own standards—and sometimes that means that I pass as a woman. Honestly? I love that. So ... I'm nonbinary, but I'm not genderqueer.
>
> I chose to pass in part because I didn't want to get beaten up. I chose to pass because all my life it's been something I've wanted—to live as a woman—and by walking through the world looking like one, I have that last handhold on the illusion, the fantasy, the dream of it all. Passing is seductive—people don't look at you like you're some kind of freak.

There's a deep shame involved in any failure to pass. As I was preparing the first draft of this book back in 1993, someone I know only peripherally came over to my house on an errand—he was with an ex-lover of mine. In casual conversation, he slipped on a pronoun and referred to me as "he."

Let me tell you what happened, the way it looked from inside my head. The world slowed down, like it does in the movies when someone is getting shot and the filmmaker wants you to feel every bullet enter your body. The word echoed in my ears over and over and over. Attached to that simple pronoun was the word *failure*, quickly followed by the word *freak*. All the joy sucked out of my life in that instant, and every moment I'd ever fucked up crashed down on my head. Here was someone who'd never known me as a man, referring to me as a man. Instead of saying or doing anything, I shut down and was polite to him for the rest of the time he was in my house.

Now here's a telling point: all three of us (as I later found out) were aware of that slip, and none of us said anything. *He's* a trained sex worker, with a great deal of experience working with sexual and gender minorities. *She* had two transsexual lovers, me having been one of them. We all knew he'd slipped on a pronoun, and none of us said anything—not a giggle, not an "oops," not one comment. Each of us was far too embarrassed to say anything 'til the next day. What does that say about the gender imperative? I think it says everything.

All of us, even the most "real-looking" trans people, embody both male and female physical characteristics. On some level, all of us are a blend. Most cisgender people miss the most subtle ways we blend gendered characteristics, because most cisgender people assume that everyone who looks cisgender is cisgender. So, who does read us? People whose identity hinges on the need to determine gender: gays and lesbians for sexual reasons, sex workers and street people for economic reasons, children for the reason of trying to establish their own place in the system.

Passing emphatically equals membership, and passing includes all the privileges of gender membership. There is most certainly a privilege to having a gender. Just ask someone who doesn't have a gender, or who can't pass, or who doesn't pass, or who doesn't want to pass. When you have a gender, or when you are perceived as having one of the two approved genders, you don't get laughed at in the street. You don't get beat up. In most cases, you know which public bathroom to use, and when you use it, people don't stare at you or worse. You know which form to fill out. You know what clothes to wear. You have heroes and role models. You have a past.

Passing by choice can be fantastic fun. Enforced passing is a joyless activity. Any joy that might be generated by the passing cannot be shared. Similarly, the joy of history lies in its telling and in its relevance to current times and relationships. Transgender people who choose or opt for a stealth life path (not revealing any previous gender or transition) are not allowed any history beyond their current gender. Denied the opportunity to speak our stories, stealth trans people are denied the joy of our histories. Sometimes it's painful for me to recall having been male: I did some stupid stuff—but that's part of me, and I need my male past as a reference point in my life. Discouraged from examining our past, trans people are discouraged from growth.

> The biggest gift for me after having gone through my gender change was getting back in touch with people I'd known when I was a guy. I really thought I'd never hear from them again. I thought they'd all think I was too weird to be in touch with. One by one, as I get back in touch with folks from my past, I can measure the continuity of my life. And I'm so grateful for their open minds and their open hearts.

The concept of passing is built into the culture's definition of transsexuality; and the result is that transsexuals don't question the gender system that their very existence could topple. Instead, through the mandate of passing, the culture uses transsexuals to reinforce the binary gender system, as transsexuals strive for recognition within their new gender, and thus the privilege and chains of their new gender.

Ironically, the concept of passing invites and even demands the concept of reading (seeing through someone else's attempt at passing) and being read. The culture desires and will insist upon an unmasking; the culture will have its "truth." The fear of being read as transsexual weighs so heavily on an individual that it focuses even more attention on "passing." It's a conundrum, because more and better passing brings about an increased fear of being read. I know too many trans men and trans women who deny their lives as trans for the sake of appearing "real."

> Passing has always been linked to "being real." And now, with the huge explosion of visible trans people in the world, views on passing are shifting. It's no longer imperative to "look real" in order to "be real."

11. What about the cultural exploitation of trans people?

I think it's inevitable, I think it's not unique to trans folks, and I think it will continue only to the degree we allow it to continue. Most marginalized people have been exoticized by some dominant culture. A dominant culture, to be truly dominant, needs its freak populations—be they racial, religious, or gender minorities, or whatever. True exploitation involves the appropriation of marginalized voices.

In the nineteenth century, one venue for the exoticization of minorities was the North American traveling medicine show. It worked like this: the manager of the show wanted to make money by selling some goods. This manager would gather up a group of exotics—usually people of color, and indigenous peoples, or people with physical anomalies (including hermaphrodites)—publicize the attributes of these "freaks," and then charge admission for the general public to come into some tent to look at them. Then the barker would launch into a talk about the exhibited minority person, or freak. The freak would say nothing, or would recite some rehearsed speech approved by the barker, who had a stake in maintaining the dehumanization of the freak so he could charge more money. The barker would proceed to sell his goods, making a double nickel from the attendees.

In the late twentieth century, there's a similar venue: the television talk show. The barker, or host, still parades the freaks out in front of the audience, but here's the big difference: it's the *sponsor* who sells the goods during the commercial break. The division of labor between barker-as-host and salesperson-as-sponsor has allowed for a whole new window of opportunity for the freak. Because the TV talk show host (barker) is not the person *directly* interested in sales, he or she can afford to be somewhat more interested in the guests (freaks). The talk show host has a stake in a ratings number, not the number of bottles of snake oil sold, so the host/barker can afford to be more sensitive and caring about the guests/freaks. The good television talk show host realizes that he or she has a stake in emphasizing the *humanity* of the guests so that the viewing audience can better identify with them. As a result, the freaks have an opportunity to speak their own words—for the first time, and to a broad audience! In this culture, I'm a freak—that's why I respected and enjoyed doing the talk shows. The television talk shows were precursors to today's reality TV, which puts even more agency into the hands of marginalized people who are seen as freaks by the dominant culture.

> I love freaks. I really do. I always have.
> When I was a young boy, my father took me to the circus. I don't remember any-

thing about the circus performance. All I remember is the sideshow. And what I remember most is Olaf, the world's tallest man. He was so tall, I had to stretch my neck way back in order to see all of him. He wore a brown suit. I remember that part. His feet were as long as my arm. He was quiet. He had . . . dignity. But his hands—damn, his hands were enormous. On each of his fingers, he wore rings, which he sold as souvenirs. I remember I was standing up front, close to his stage, as he spoke of his life. I didn't understand a word he said, but I worshipped him. And then he bent down toward me. His already immense head grew larger and larger as his face drew near to mine. And I remember no fear. He knew me, and I knew him. He smiled. I smiled. Then he took one of the rings off his finger and put it around my wrist. And I knew I was just like him. I knew I was a freak.

Freaks always know that.

I love doing television talk shows—I respect the format. I'm a child of television, so I'm familiar with the venue, and I've learned the language of sound bites. Unlike Olaf, I don't need some barker to approve my material before I present it. I can have fun bantering with the host and parrying questions and answers with the audience. And I can usually get back to the single point I want to make on that show.

When a politician appears on a talk show, they are called media-savvy. When I appear on a talk show, I'm called self-centered, self-serving, and a freak. Go figure.

In every medium, there's a comfortable, three-way symbiosis among the talk show hosts, their guests, and their audiences. The relationship between host and guest is a tacit understanding of the need to communicate to the largest possible number of viewers, and to fulfill some "social service" obligation of information dissemination. It's theater, and both host and guest play a role, one in agreement with the other. The relationship between the two of them and the audience is more magical—like the magic between a young child and a circus giant.

"It's Pat" was a *Saturday Night Live* comedy skit that ran for four years, from 1990 through 1994. Julia Sweeney played Pat, a baffling androgynous character. No one could attribute male or female to Pat. When I first heard about the skit, I thought it was a great idea, but I figured the joke would be on all the characters who were desperate to determine Pat's gender. Instead, the joke was consistently on Pat, who is shown as a slobbering, unattractive, simpering nerd. Pat, of course, *cannot* be attractive, because that would return gender ambiguity to its apparently rightful place of being desirable, and that's simply too dangerous. When it came out, most trans people considered "It's Pat" to be mean-spirited and transphobic. Video clips are still being posted to YouTube. Go look for yourself.

Transgender is only now in a position to say, "To fuck with me is politically incorrect and social suicide, so hands off." Civil rights groups now defend trans men and women, and every day more and more people and groups are coming together to support all trans people, including genderqueer, agender, and otherwise gender-nonconforming people.

12. Is there a role for the trans folks in this culture?

Many post-transition trans people don't want a role as trans—they're happy with their new roles as men and women. As for the rest of us, I don't believe it's up to the culture to create such a role. I think it's up to gender outlaws to claim one for ourselves. Our culture, some say, has no place for not-men, not-women.

There are some who point to other cultures with envy. These other cultures, they say, have established roles for those who break the rules of gender. Hijras in India, for example, call themselves "neither men nor women." Their role in Indian culture is a spiritual one, presiding over marriages and births. Traditionally, hijra has been a despised identity, shunned and abused. Nevertheless, more hijras refused to give up their identities and assimilate into a binary gender system. And their stubborn insistence on their authentic genders has paid off. After thousands of years, India, along with Pakistan and Australia, now legally acknowledges three genders.

Whereas Westerners feel uncomfortable with the ambiguities and contradictions inherent in such in-between categories as transvestism, homosexuality, hermaphroditism, and transgenderism, and make strenuous attempts to resolve them, Hinduism not only accommodates such ambiguities, but also views them as meaningful and even powerful.

—Serena Nanda, Neither Man Nor Woman:
The Hijras of India, *1990*

Our Western culture has little room for gender in any shade of gray, so it wouldn't make much sense to expect this binary culture to create a role for people whose very existence threatens the binary. The trans shamans of other cultures earned their roles; their roles as guides and healers were not doled out to them. Similarly, today's not-men, not-women must earn a position in today's culture. That place in the world will certainly not be a gift to us. Left to fate, the roles we have been gifted with in today's culture have been roles of shame and death.

It would be important that any role gender outlaws wind

up claiming is not a role that would by its very existence forward the culture that oppresses transgender and related borderwalkers.

> » Any us-versus-them position forwards a culture that oppresses transgender. Opt rather for a role that is inclusive and promotes inclusion.
> » Any position that operates nonconsensually (violently) forwards a culture that oppresses transgender. Choose only positions that trade in degrees of agreement and consent.
> » Any power-over position forwards a culture that oppresses transgender. We should look for positions that allow us to bring out the power we have within us and to acknowledge the power of others.

13. You say you want a revolution?

Over the past twenty-five years, trans people have increasingly been speaking in their own voice. It's the beginnings of a revolution.

> The problem with revolution, of course, is violence. It would be neat to take part in a nonviolent revolution of inclusion, whereby the revolutionaries simply have a good laugh and welcome anyone else to dinner. Ah, I am such a hippie.

Guess Who's Coming to the Revolution?

In defining the left and right wings of the gender discourse, one need only look at who has an investment in the binary gender system for the sake of their identity. Any revolution in deconstructing gender should look for *no* support among communities of people whose identities depend on the existence of this binary gender system. This would include, but most certainly is not limited to, the fundamentalist right wing, purists in the lesbian and gay male communities who believe in the ultimate goal of assimilation into the dominant culture, and some cultural or radical feminists. Nonsupporters of any movement to deconstruct gender would also, unfortunately, include those transgender people who subscribe fully to the culture's definitions of gender and seek to embody those definitions within themselves.

> Judeo-Christian fundamentalists, trans-excluding radical feminists, and assimilationist transgender activists all seem to be united against the theory that you don't **have** to be a man or a woman. I wanted to find out what they have in common. When I looked deeper than their common need for a fixed gender, it hit me that we're talking about an old, old philosophical conflict here: we're talking order versus chaos—some people need one or the other. In our postmodern global village, order and chaos could very well be used to define the real right wing (order, aka **straight**) and left wing (chaos, aka **queer**) of any discourse.

Heterosexuals and homosexuals alike demand the need for an orderly gender system: they're two sides of the same coin, each holding the other in place, neither willing to dismantle the gender system that serves as a matrix for their (sexual) identity. Because of the binary nature of both sexual orientation and gender in the dominant paradigm, one system strengthens the other. Bisexuality and androgyny also hold two sides in place by defining themselves as somewhere in the middle of two given polar opposites.

Arthur J. Deikman maintains that it is important to devalue those outside the group. In terms of marginal queer culture, the irony is all too clear. Lesbians, gay men, and other queer people first burst into the world as self-defined outlaws. "We are not like you," they said to the heterosexual culture. Today, many former outlaws paradoxically wish to exist within the very culture that defines us as outsiders, and this is the beginning of assimilationism.

In order to reinforce their newly included position within the dominant ideology, assimilationist lesbians, gays, bisexuals, and transgender people must accept the rules and the boundaries of the straight culture—and so they become straight-identified, needing to cast as outsiders those who would threaten the integrity of their membership. They need to disown their own. This is called heteronormativity and cisnormativity. In contrast, the more radically identified dykes, fags, pansexuals, and genderqueers renounce any rules of binary sexuality and gender. It's these queer people—those who would give gender deconstruction a bad name—who would probably work the hardest for that deconstruction. It's the straight-identified people who would lend "respectability" to the notion of trans who would never work toward it.

Who Are the Allies?

Transgendered people are mistakenly viewed as the cusp of the lesbian and

gay community. In reality the two huge
communities are like circles that only
partially overlap.

—Leslie Feinberg, Transgender Liberation: A
Movement Whose Time Has Come, 1992

If we're going to work with one another to achieve rights for all, then we need to include one another in our struggles. So who gets to include whom becomes a pressing question.

The lesbian and gay community is solidifying and becoming more of a codified group—existing within and accepted by the dominant ideology. Self-defined "queers" become more and more the adversarial outsiders, the ungrateful children, the bad influence—queers like the drag queens, the stone butches, the dyke leather daddies, the she-males—the ones who are going to "wreck everything" for (assimilated) lesbians and gays. We can see this playing itself out in the letters LGBTQ. The addition of the letter Q very plainly states that LGB and T are not queer. And if something isn't queer, well, it's more or less straight. And so LGBT is establishing itself as the more or less straight arm of the sex and gender revolution.

Assuming that gay men and lesbians are more consciously excluded by the culture for violations of *gender* codes (which are visible in the daily life of the culture) than for actual sexual practices (which usually happen behind closed doors and in private spaces), then lesbians and gay men actually share the same stigma with trans people: the stigma of crimes against gender.

Until recently, trans activists used the word *transgender* as an identity that was inclusive of anyone messing around with gender so as to be more inclusive. Transgender used to mean "transgressively gendered." At this writing, *trans* is that inclusive word. In trans, we have people who break the rules, codes, and shackles of gender—as well as people who follow the rules. That's a healthy-sized contingent! It's trans who can embrace the lesbians and gays—not the other way around—because it's trans who are in fact the more inclusive category.

Of course, this will offend everyone. It will seem to negate and belittle the hard-won gains of lesbians and gay men. It will seem to make invisible the bisexuals. It will seem to dilute a supposedly unique transgender struggle. But it's the only point all these groups have in common, it's the only flag around which they all can rally. Failing one great big happy family under one great big happy name, we need to at least stop attacking one another.

It's going to be difficult. For lesbians and gays to include transgender people, or indeed be included by them, would require that gays and lesbians admit to what amounts to their own trans status: that of breaking the rules "real men love women and real women love men." It would require a questioning of sexual identity, which is currently based solely on the gender of their desired partners. That's a lot to ask, but I think that competent and compassionate negotiators from marginalized sexual and gender camps could get together and come up with some inclusive name. Lesbians and gay men today stand at a crossroads with bisexuals and trans people, said Leslie Feinberg. Further down the road, we're going to need all the community we can muster when it comes time to stand at the crossroads against patriarchal oppression. Only our bonding will permit a true revolution of sex and gender.

14. Where's the fun?

All roads in life lead nowhere. So you might as well take the road that has the most heart and is the most fun.

—Anonymous Zen saying

It's frightening to be genderless. What makes it easier is a sense of humor, and that's where *camp* comes into the picture. Camp is a uniquely queer experience. It's a sense of humor developed in response to oppression based on a unique gender identity, and a minority sexual orientation.

It is possible to discern strong themes in any particular campy thing or event. The three that seemed most recurrent and characteristic to me were **incongruity**, **theatricality**, *and* **humor**. *All three are intimately related to the homosexual situation and strategy. Incongruity is the subject matter of camp, theatricality its style, and humor its strategy.*

—*Esther Newton,* Mother Camp: Female Impersonators in America, 1979

Camp thumbs its nose at the straight world, lampooning and violating its rituals. Camp points out the silliness, exaggerates the roles, shines big spotlights on the gender dynamic. Camp is only possible when there is little or no fear of humiliation—and at that point, social control becomes very difficult.

As theater, the Sisters of Perpetual Indulgence are electric. They cannot be ignored. The minute they **appear** *on the scene, the atmosphere is charged with humor, hostility, disgust—but rarely indifference.*

—*Kevin Starr,* "Indulging the Sisters," The San Francisco Examiner, 1981

When we think of camp, we usually think of gay men and drag queens, but they aren't the only ones who lampoon the culture's definition of women and men. As early as the late 1980s, performers like Dominique Dibbell, member of the Five Lesbian Brothers, have taken both girl and boy drag onto the stage.

I enjoy doing feminine drag—female drag. It was a great revolution when femmes started to come out and say that we could embrace this way of looking—this femme role—and be powerful and sexy and attractive to women; and still be 100 percent lesbian. That's always exciting for me to see and to perform. The **male** *drag thing has always been a traditionally lesbian thrill, and it still is. Male drag is very sexy, and that's what it's about. There's just something about putting a masculine wrapper on a female body—you just want to take the wrapper off!*

—Dominique Dibbell, personal interview
with the author, 1993

Some folks think that camp, or drag in general, is an attempt to ape or become the dominant culture. What I learned to see once I got off the straight and narrow road was this: camp performers were taking pieces of the culture and twisting them around to a point of humor, and then and only then wearing the scalps (wigs) of their oppressors as badges of victory.

High camp can be a person in full nun drag, with great showgirl makeup, on roller-skates in the middle of town. Does that person really want to be a Catholic nun?

Camp has always been with us. It's had other names in other times; and other leanings in other cultures. In India, for example, there exists an old tradition of jesters, *Bhands*, or *bahurupiya*. Their function in the Rajasthan caste society seems quite similar to the function of camp performers in today's Eurocentric culture.

As a joker in the deck, a "wild card" in an otherwise carefully labeled pack, the **bahurupiya** *serves as a reminder that even in the most rigid societies, identities are not fixed. The wheel of karma takes many turns; a prince in one cycle may find himself a pauper in another as the* **lila**—*or play—of life continues.*

—John Emigh, "Hajari Bhand of Rajasthan: A
Joker in the Deck," The Drama Review, 1986

Camp can be a leading edge in the deconstruction of gender, because camp wrests social control from the hands of the fanatics. Camp and drag in fact reclaim gender and reshape it as a consensual game. Setting about to do away with gender could itself turn into a frighteningly fanatical mission. Fanatics are distinguishable by the fact that they can't laugh at themselves. Camp and drag are the safety valves that can keep any gender activism from becoming fanaticism.

In doing away with a binary gender system, one needn't do away with playing at genders. Drag is fun! Mainstream drag performers like Lady Gaga and Arnold Schwarzenegger have opened doors for all of us. Lady G is the consummate drag queen. Arnold Schwarzenegger does male drag perfectly! Miley Cyrus and Ruby Rose are pioneering nonbinary (genderqueer) drag in the mainstream.

15. What about the future of gender?

Many trans people are living the future of gender right now. What's more, the future of gender is available to anyone who wants to dive into any number of virtual realities. Although the term conjures up visions of Google Cardboard and augmented reality, I like a broader definition of virtual reality, which would embrace any representation of reality, including gaming, the written word, telephone, Twitter, Tumblr, and the great, grand ancestor of all virtual realities: theater.

Theater is [Brenda] Laurel's metaphor for virtual reality. In a field with almost no historical perspective, she draws on thousands of years of theatrical analysis. To Laurel, the V[irtual] R[eality] user is an actor, playing off other actors, taking action, exploring characters, experimenting with appearances, behavior, or gender. "Reality has always been too small for the human imagination. We're always trying to transcend," Laurel says.
  —Susan McCarthy, "Techno Soaps and Virtual Theatre," Wired, 1993

Gender is a method of partitioning our identities, our families, our economics, or our society. Virtual reality is a method of making partitions obsolete. We have the opportunity to play with gender in much the same way that we get to play with other forms of identity—through performance in any virtual medium. In any medium, there have always been cross-gendered performances.

When I was a phone sex hostess, I knew many hostesses who were men, and several of us were trans women. The actual gender of the hostesses didn't matter, as long as they could act. Phone sex was theater. We hostesses were playing our roles, for which we'd get paid. In turn, the clients played their roles, for which opportunity they'd pay us.

More sophisticated virtual realities allow for more opportunities to play with gender, as well as more sophisticated methods of playing, but any virtual reality is a playing field on which we can rehearse for the future.

Ever since the inception of interacting online, there have always been men who are online as women. Similarly, I've known many women who've gone online as men. Me, I've gone online as straight women, bisexual women, and lesbian women. I haven't given much thought to going online as a man—I've had all the male experience I'd like, thank you very much.

The futures of gender, spirituality, and virtual reality are converging, here in the first couple of decades of the current millennium. If we begin, in virtual reality, to render partitions as needless, or at best as boundaries for some consensual game, then we have the opportunity to carry that skill over into our day-to-day worlds.

Now What?

Having asked some questions, it's time to explore the possibilities that the questions have raised. Any theory is only meaningful if it can be put to use, and it should be possible to apply these principles in a more or less measurable arena. Fortunately, gender is so pervasive in the culture that there are an infinite number of circumstances for playing with it, and, after raising the questions, it will be the act of playing with gender that's going to change cultural attitudes about gender. We bring about the future of gender when we put gender into play in any aspect of our daily lives: family, work, play, or relationship. It's when we put gender into play, it's when we question the binary, it's when we break the rules and keep calling attention to the fact that the rules are breakable: that's when we create a Third Space. I've been putting gender into play in theater, and it was through theater that I discovered how to apply this theory. My queer theater was my Third Space.

Yearbook photo, 1969

creating a third space

I think it's up to each transgressively gendered person to create a space for this life as Third. At home, at play, and at work. My workplace is the theater, and while there is a lot of theater about folks like us, there is relatively little space for us in person. Like other transgressively gendered folks, I'm managing to get a foot in the door; my door is the stage door, that's all.

On the **Geraldo** segment "Transsexual Regrets: Who's Sorry Now?" I was the one who **wasn't** sorry.

13

TRANSSEXUAL LESBIAN PLAYWRIGHT TELLS ALL!

Written as a talk for the Out/Write '90 conference of lesbian and gay writers, in San Francisco, and adapted for inclusion in volume one of the anthology **High Risk**.

My ancestors were performers. In life. The earliest shamanic rituals involved women and men exchanging genders. Old, old rituals. Top-notch performances. Life and death stuff. We're talking cross-cultural here. We're talking rising way way way above being a man or a woman. That's how my ancestors would fly. That's how my ancestors would talk with the goddesses and the gods. Old rituals.

I'd been a performer of one sort or another for over twenty-five years, and now I'm writing plays as well as performing in them. See, I had never seen my story onstage and I was looking. I used to go up to writers I knew. I used to wish they'd write my story. And I'm only just now realizing that they couldn't possibly. I write from the point of view of an S/M transsexual lesbian, ex-cult member, femme top, and sometimes bottom shaman. And I wondered why no one was writing my story? I'm writing from the point of view of used-to-be-a-man, three husbands, father, first mate on an oceangoing yacht, minister, high-powered IBM sales type, Pierre Cardin three-piece suitor, bar mitzvahed, circumcised yuppie from the East Coast. Not too many women write from that point of view. I write from the point of view of a used-to-be politically correct, wannabe butch, dyke phone sex hostess, smooth talking, telemarketing, love slave, art slut, pagan tarot reader, maybe soon a grandmother, crystal palming, incense burning, not-man, not always a woman, fast becoming a Marxist. And not too many men write from that point of view.

My ancestors didn't write much. I guess they didn't need to.

Y'know, people try to write about transsexuals and it's amusing it's infuriating it's patronizing and it's why *I'm* writing about transsexuals now. I wrote one play in college twenty-one years ago. And one play last year. Both of them I pulled from my chest until they pulsed bleeding onto the stage. Saint Kate of the bleeding heart. The first play was young love gone bad. Spun out my soul as just so much cotton candy romanticism. God it felt great. The second play was a harder birth. *Hidden: A Gender* is my transsexual voice—the voice I speak with, cry with, roar with, moan with, and laugh with, don't forget laugh with. I always hid that voice away. I always used your voice, spoke your words, sang your hit parade. Until I heard them whisper, my ancestors. And I whispered and you heard me and I said hey you weren't meant to hear that and you said tell us more. And that was the second play, the harder birth. The one I had to write.

I write when nothing else will bring me peace, when I burn, when I find myself asking and answering the same questions over and over. I write when I've begun to lose my sense of humor and it becomes a matter of my life and my death to get that sense of humor back and watch you laugh. I write in bottom space. I open up to you, I cut myself, I show you my fantasies, I get a kick out of that—oh, yeah. I perform in top space. I cover myself with my character and take you where you never dreamed you could go. Yes. My ancestors did this. My instrument is not my pen or my typewriter, not my lover's Macintosh, not my cast of characters, not my body onstage. No, my instrument is my audience and oh how I love to play you.

And to what end? I've come to see gender as a divisive social construct, and the gendered body as a somewhat dubious accomplishment. I write about this because I am a gender outlaw and my issues are gender issues. The way I see it now, the lesbian and gay community is as much oppressed for gender transgressions as for sexual distinction. We have more in common, you and I, than most people are willing to admit. See, I'm told I must be a man or a woman. One or the other. Oh, it's okay to be a trans-sexual, say some—just don't talk about it. Don't question your gender any more, just be a woman now—you went to so much trouble—just be satisfied. I am so not satisfied. My ancestors were not satisfied.

I write from the point of view of a gender outlaw because I don't want to hear: We don't want you in our club / We don't want you on our land / We don't want you in our march. And I say I don't know why the separatists won't let me in—I'm *probably* the only lesbian to have successfully castrated a man and gone on to laugh about it onstage, in print, and on national television.

Hello, Geraldo, are you reading this?

My ancestors were not shunned. They were celebrated. Look, I know you try to fill in the blanks in my life. I write to let you know who I am so that you *can* fill in the blanks.

Hello, Mom, are you reading this?

Anyway, I work in theater because I really enjoy working *with* people, and theater is not an alone art. And current theatrical forms reflect a rigidly bi-polar gender system. They aren't fluid enough for what I want to say, and I feel that form and content in theater as in life should be complementary, not adversarial, so I work on my own gender fluidity and sometimes it works and sometimes it doesn't. And I work on the fluidity of my theatrical style—and sometimes it works and sometimes it doesn't. My life and my theater—my form and my content—sort of do as I say and do as I do. Like my ancestors.

—*San Francisco, March 1990*

Promotional photo for the first production of Hidden: A Gender, *directed by Noreen C. Barnes. (top to bottom) Kate Bornstein, Sydney Erskine, Justin Bond.*

14

QUEER LIFE/QUEER THEATER

I've tweaked a good deal of the text in this new edition in order to bring it more up to date in context with the increasingly nuanced ways we look at gender. Queer theater continues to evolve, and I am enjoying the work of today's queer theater artists. But I'm letting this chapter stand pretty much as it was written, because I think it gives a good picture of what our queer theater was like in the United States in the 1980s and 1990s—it's what I knew and how I knew to write about it. Okay, here we go back in time ...

I see theater as the performance of identity, which is acknowledged as a performance. We're always performing identities, but when we consciously perform one, and people acknowledge our performance, it's theater. When people hone the skill of that performance to a point where other people will actually pay to see them do it, the skilled people are called actors or performers or theater artists, and they can charge admission.

The two things I thought I'd have to give up by going through my gender change were orgasms and theater.

See, my surgeon warned me that I might

have no more sensation in my genitals after surgery—that I may never have another orgasm.

My own insecurity insisted that I'd never be able to perform onstage again. I mean, who would ever cast me? What kind of role could I play? There were few enough parts for women—but a not-man, not-woman like me? I was a freak, and there was no place for me in the theater I'd grown up with and trained in. I went through my gender change anyway—a stable gender identity mattered that much more at the time.

As it turned out, I never got a stable gender identity. I did end up, however, with both orgasms and theater.

As individuals express their life, so they are.

—Karl Marx

Growing up, I saw no theater that mirrored my trans life, my patchwork gender. I wanted to express my life through my chosen work, but it just wasn't being done, so, like a chameleon, I lived my theatrical life day to day, rather than putting it up on the stage. I learned to live my life like I'm making a collage, and my theater follows that pattern. My queer theater consists of elements I gather along the way.

Speaking, my accent still echoes this chameleon quality—you can hear in me traces of New Jersey, New York, Toronto, Alabama,

California, Philadelphia, and London by way
of Saskatoon.

First and Second Theaters

My experience in theater is grounded in naturalism and the
Aristotelian model. I grew up with Eugene O'Neill, Tennessee
Williams, Lillian Hellman, and that gang—lots of reach-into-
your-guts-and-pull-out-the-still-beating-heart; but I was looking
to pull rabbits out of my hat. I found theatrical magic in Broad-
way musicals, people suddenly bursting into song at their most
emotional moments.

In college, I waded through the identity politics of Albee and
LeRoi Jones, without ever really discovering their identities. I
stumbled over the magical unrealism of Brecht, Artaud, Jarry, and
Beckett, but I was too stoned to incorporate their styles into my
work at the time. Despite that, I was usually involved in the more
conservative student theater organizations and productions—the
Aristotelian model of conflict/resolution and moral integrity was
the only theater I studied in depth, a theater designed to teach
morality to a generally immoral theatergoing audience. It wasn't
until very recently that I had the luxury of really being able to
study alternate forms of theater.

> In 1969, I broke ranks and joined Judith
> Malina and Julian Beck for a few days in the
> Living Theater Company—my photograph
> graces the pages of **Playboy** magazine,
> August 1969: I'm bending over, my back-
> side to the camera, wearing only my jockey
> shorts. A close friend of mine, Gail Harris,
> convinced me to leave the Living Theater
> and return to finish college.

My life drifted lazily between classes, rehearsals, performances, relationships, and drugs. I got it that I could act—I would be tragic and audiences would cry, I would be comic and audiences would laugh. But none of that tragedy was mine. None of the humor came from inside me. I didn't know what was important to say or what was worth performing. As an actor and director, I felt I was someone who could interpret others' voices, but that I had no voice of my own.

"Kathy, I'm lost," I said,
though I knew she was sleeping.
"I'm empty and aching and I don't know
why—"
counting the cars on the New Jersey
Turnpike.
They've all come to look for America.
                    —Paul Simon and Art Garfunkel,
                          "America," 1968

1985: I'd just begun living part-time as a woman. The Church of Scientology, IBM, and the tatters of my third and final marriage were behind me. I drove up from Philadelphia to New York to see Charles Ludlam perform *The Mystery of Irma Vep*. I was expecting a simple drag performance. Instead, Ludlam transformed his gender onstage from male to something not exactly female— but transformed nonetheless. Ludlam incorporated elements of naturalism in his work, as well as elements of physical comedy. The result was fluid, highlighting the best of both naturalistic and magical elements.

Ludlam's multi-gendered life reverberated throughout his work: he performed from behind a fourth wall, regularly peeking out and acknowledging the presence of the audience.

In 1986, just after my genital surgery, I directed a production of Jane Chambers's *Last Summer at Bluefish Cove* for the Philadelphia-based feminist theater company Order Before Midnight. This is when I found out that some art offends some people. Our production of *Bluefish Cove* was the Philadelphia premiere of the play, but *The Philadelphia Inquirer* and the other mainstream (non-lesbian/-gay) papers refused to review us.

> Additionally, some women from the local lesbian separatist community boycotted us on the grounds that I was involved with the production. It was the first time I experienced what was to become a recurring alliance against transgender people: the conservative elements of both heterosexual and lesbian politics could find a common ground in decrying a transgender life and a transgender art.

Chambers's style was wonderfully corny, and steeped in the Aristotelian model: story line, characters who go through conflict, and a resolution. It was a portrait of lesbians, written by a lesbian, using what had previously been used to portray only a heterosexual model. The style of the piece is almost television sitcom, a style more accustomed to bashing gays than singing their praises. Chambers appropriated elements of an oppressor's art, putting them to use in the portrayal of a minority point of view. By doing that, she was able to communicate to folks who were accustomed only to a straight, naturalistic format. She didn't have to reinvent the wheel; she was free to use it in ways the wheel-makers never dreamt of. By seeing nonconventional people acting within a conventional model, the audience learns that lesbians are real people.

> Traditional form permits an audience to experience nontraditional content in relative safety.

The next component of my queer theater came from a production of *Upwardly Mobile Home*, written and performed by Split Britches, a feminist theater company from New York. Like Ludlam, Split Britches members Lois Weaver, Peggy Shaw, and Deborah Margolin shifted the *form* of their theater so that the form itself emulated a queer life. Instead of a linear story line, there were many stories woven together, each beginning and ending at different times; and instead of conflict and resolution, there was transformation.

[In our work,] we try to build in as many layers as we can, because reality isn't simple. Reality isn't just one story line. In that sense, it's possible for people to enter our work at different places, and our work becomes accessible to our audiences at different levels.

—Lois Weaver, in conversation with the author,

1989

The strength of the queer community in San Francisco in the late '80s showed up in the strength of its theater—both theater and community were out of the closet. Which came out *first* doesn't matter—it was a partnership between the community and its theater, one leading the other at different times in their mutual development. By the mid-'80s, many gay men and lesbians were not simply negotiating for assimilated positions in the culture, they were clamoring for attention, and their theater clamored along with them. Inspired by their bravery, I began to demand attention for my nonbinary trans issues. In the summer of 1988, I attended a theater conference and performed there as part of a panel. I wanted feedback.

Kate Bornstein re-creates three theater scenes out of her acting past—macho make-out artist Tolen's advice on getting birds, from Ann Jellicoe's '60s play, **The Knack**; *two bits from* **Happy End**; *a monologue from Jane Chambers'* **Last Summer at Bluefish Cove**. *Bornstein is transsexual and lesbian. When she performed in the Jellicoe play, she was still male, but says that, feeling alien to Tolen's type, s/he had to be coached to play him. Shades, leather jacket, attitude. The performance is very funny, what the audience knows bouncing off Tolen's words—"Women aren't individuals, they're types, no, not types, just women, they want to be dominated." Woman playing former male self playing male.*

Bornstein did **Happy End** *while saving money for the operation. A dual role. The director had invented an androgynous narrator/emcee à la* **Cabaret** *who also acted the female mob leader, in drag. Bornstein's San Diego performance is bittersweet, early Brecht, with an added canny mockery of drag's mockery. Woman playing former straight male self playing gay man playing straight woman. The Chambers came five months after the surgery; her re-creating is naturalistic, unlayered ex-*

cept by what we already know. I find
it ordinary after so much sex-identity
vertigo and role critique. But Bornstein
says, deadpan, "I've come to see the
gendered body as an accomplishment."
                    —*Erika Munk,* The Village Voice, *1988*

It was the first time in my life I felt I had something of my own
worth saying—something that raised questions.

Watching her perform, I was unsettled
by my awareness that Bornstein has no
neutral body, that even her biology is not
immutable but constructed. Is this the
death of character? Where is the truth
in this experience?
                    —*Jill Dolan,* The Drama Review, *1989*

Hidden: A Gender grew out of that performance. Women at the conference kept
coming up to me asking me when I was
going to perform the full-length version of
"this new piece," and they would ask me
the title. Well, the big buzzword that year
was **agenda**. Everyone was talking about
this agenda, or that agenda. I made a joke
that I had a hidden **agender**. John Emigh
encouraged me to write the piece, but I'd
never before considered writing about that
part of my life.

Around this time, Holly Hughes was performing her one-woman
show *World Without End.* Hughes performed her life with an ach-

ingly beautiful blend of humor, strength, sarcasm, and vulnerability. Using pieces of her very personal life, she spoke onstage
what had been forbidden in polite conversation. That was the key
I needed to begin writing my own work. Hers was the artistic
courage I was looking for. I'd been working diligently at blurring
the lines between male and female, the cultural binary of gender.
Watching Hughes perform, I realized it's both possible and necessary to blur the lines of another culturally constructed binary:
life and art. I wrote *Hidden: A Gender*, and it was coproduced by
Theatre Rhinoceros and Outlaw Productions.

> If it's been bottled up inside you for a long
> time, if it's been gnawing at every hour of
> your life, if it makes you cringe to think that
> people might find out, it would probably
> make a great piece of theater.

Work is love made visible.

—*Kahlil Gibran*

A Cavalcade of Stars:
Live (For Now) on the Queer Stage!

> **Hidden: A Gender** was selected to
> represent Theatre Rhinoceros at the first
> International Lesbian and Gay Theater
> Conference and Festival, sponsored by the
> Alice B. Theatre in Seattle. "Selected" might
> be too kind a word. A play called **Lust and
> Pity** was actually selected, but in the true
> style of Mickey Rooney, Judy Garland, and

'40s musicals, the cast of **Lust and Pity** couldn't make it, and so, like Mickey and Judy, we were on.

The first International Lesbian and Gay Theater Conference and Festival took place within days of the announcement by John Frohnmayer, then Chairman of the U.S. National Endowment for the Arts, that the Endowment would be rescinding grants to a number of artists who had been judged by their peers as deserving of that money.

We'd been told all our lives that we were bad and undeserving, and despite that, we did our art, brought our lives into the open—only to be told by some faceless power structure that our lives, our work, were indeed bad and indeed undeserving.

There's a real chance for a blacklist these days. A real chance. It's apparent in the lack of response from the Left to the Right's blatant appeal to homophobia. They want us dead.

*As to my NEA grant being rescinded, people call me and they say, "This will be the best thing for your career, Holly," and I say, Fuck you! Fuck you! Be **me** for a day!*

—Holly Hughes

What's convenient for the government is that they keep getting this scapegoat called the queer voice. Hey—silence

*does equal death, and we are si-
lenced. And you know the scary part?
The scary part is that the people voting
on this haven't even seen the work—
they're reading lies. The majority of
people are reading lies.*

—Lori E. Seid, at a panel at the first
International Lesbian and Gay Theater
Conference and Festival, 1989

Censorship became the buzzword, and nearly, but not quite, the entire focus of the conference. We tried to figure out ways to get the work done—in spite of the efforts to silence us.

*Holly is not exaggerating—they do
want us dead. The what-is-to-be-done
question looms large for me, and what
I'm afraid of is that this period will sig-
nal self-censorship to young artists. We
need to continue to blur the lines—find
common ground with each other—
continue to open possibilities for cultural
exchange. And we need to develop a
sort of underground railroad of performance spaces for lesbians and gays to
do their work. Well—if they can't get
grants, they can get work.*

—Tim Miller, at a panel at the first
International Lesbian and Gay Theater
Conference and Festival, 1989

*This year, it's the solo lesbian and gay
artists. Next year, it will be the organizations called lesbian and gay. The following*

*year, it will be the groups and institutions that systematically **hire** lesbian and gay artists that have been refused grants. You get the picture—the line is creeping up.*

We need all of us to keep saying the words lesbian *and* gay. *We have to educate people that we exist and that we are amazing! We have to come out and reach out with our work. We **have** to come out.*

—Susan Finque, at a panel at the first International Lesbian and Gay Theater Conference and Festival, 1989

I'm a reluctant activist. I prefer calling myself an artist in service to activism. My reluctance comes from the sad fact that even after the lesbian and gay revolution is over and won, there are going to be people dumping on me as a transsexual, or for being into S/M. I want to give my power to a movement that will speak *my* name as well.

At the conference, I found a theater with the potential to include anyone who will wear the name "queer"; and that includes me as both a transsexual and as an S/M dyke. We were united at that time against this seemingly monolithic oppressor, the U.S. government, which was coming down heavily on queer folks by trying to wipe out our artists.

When I was first writing this, there was a new president in the White House, things were looking up for queers, and it was only as the final draft of this book was being prepared that the government agreed to settle and make restitution to the artists for wrongs done by the NEA under the Reagan and Bush administrations.

Part of the reason queer theater is inclusive is because it's had to be—
we face a common oppression, and we need to unite against it.

How do we know how to seek out and learn about other gay people when they are so invisible, so ridiculed and diminished by everything that we see and hear? The effeminate man has been, and remains, the laughingstock of our movies, our most successful comedians. The butch woman is an object of particular scorn—but then, all women are.

Homophobia and misogyny are not related. THEY ARE THE SAME! The man who makes an object of himself is beneath contempt. And the woman who refuses to be one must be stopped. The fact that we wish to be ourselves and choose our same [gender] as partners is the most threatening idea to those who will never examine themselves.

—Craig Lucas, at a panel at the first International Lesbian and Gay Theater Conference and Festival, 1989

Sex and gender outlaws have needed allies. An empowering theater is a strong partner: a space in which people can work together for a common goal of freedom. Queer theater has been inclusive going a long way back. Lesbians, gay men, bisexuals, trans folks, S/Mers, all trace their roots to early cultures' shamanic rituals of transformation. These shamans were the healers, the mystics, the channelers of the truth of their time. They were the tricksters, the jokers and jesters and poets; they were the whores and the priestesses. As whores and poets, they traded in love.

What's important is loving the audience.
It's not about what you feel as a per-
former when you're up there—it's not
about your personal catharsis. As an au-
dience member, I want you to make **me**
feel something. That's why I come to the
theater. The artists I have the most re-
spect for, and I'm most moved by, are
those who give so much of their hearts.
To me, a good performance is, in its es-
sence, an act of love.

—David Harrison,
in correspondence with the author, 1993

As jesters and priestesses, our queer ancestors traded in the healing arts.

What we do is we choose stereotypes
as characters, but then we inhabit them
as performers. And we twist these ste-
reotypes, because that's what happens
when you inhabit what has hurt you.
There's something very healing about
loving the people who have hurt you the
most, and then literally taking them on.
It's a way the world can help itself.

—Deborah Margolin,
in conversation with the author, 1989

Our ancestors played around with gender, as well as with sexuality. And their rituals were theater. Our ancestors performed
their rituals, their theater, to heal themselves, and to heal their
tribes. I *like* that heritage—it's one I don't mind trying to live
up to.

It's strange how that heritage has become buried. It's strange that while there are so many queer people in theater, the institution of mainstream misogynist theater is, like most of today's world, homophobic and transphobic, and so the queer people in theater stay to themselves. They become isolated.

I was always fascinated with the relationship between the spiritual and the theatrical. Raised a conservative Jew, I nearly converted to Catholicism, so drawn was I to their ritual theater. But just as neither conservative Judaism nor conservative Catholicism speaks to me or for me these days, a conservative theater also frustrates me. Theater that grows up in a community, with the aim of supporting that community, will become a theater that pacifies its audience. Its aim will be to preserve, and it will not provoke rebellion, but rather promote the community's status quo. In the same way that a fool and a shaman must, for their continued survival, stay free of attachment to any community, so must a theater stay free of any attachment to a community.

Some of the most skillful theater I've seen is cranked out these days for the church of consumerism. This art is commissioned in the name of advertising and public relations. Maybe several hundred years from now, we'll look back on this art and really appreciate its beauty apart from its politics, just as today we admire works of art commissioned by the Catholic Church hundreds of years ago. But remember that church work was commissioned to keep people in the fold of Catholicism. Similarly, today's advertising art is commissioned to keep people nestled deep within the fold of materialism.

In choosing to break from the patron church of capitalism, the queer artists at this conference found themselves seriously under-funded, underpaid, and alone. A number of queer theater art-ists expressed the feeling that the conference was "home." That they'd met their own kind. That it was family.

The problem is, we've been doing our work in isolation from one another. A lot of us became aware we can't do that any more. We're not in competition with each other like in straight theater—we do tend to work together, and we gain so much more. The topics we talk about may be different, but we are united in style. The style, or structural device, seems to be a blending of genres into one piece.

—Noreen C. Barnes, at a panel at the first International Lesbian and Gay Theater Conference and Festival, 1989

As outlaws—lesbians, gay men, transgender, bisexual, or as S/M players—we lampoon the images of the dominant (i.e., hetero-normative) culture. We blend, fold, and mutilate popular forms and genres and claim them for ourselves. The end result is oddly cohesive and coherent. Camp, drag, and dyke noire drama are all examples of this mélange of barbed comedy.

I learned about theater from a group of drag queens in a theater company called Hot Peaches, way back when. I learned a lifestyle of sharing and healthy competition. Where being good meant you had to wear higher heels, sew more sequins onto your costume, and dye your hair a funnier color than anyone else's. Succeeding meant stepping in front of somebody else onstage so you could be seen, and talking louder than somebody else so you could be heard.

*And I finally said to all these guys, "Hey, there's no material here about women in this group." And they looked at me and said, "So, what's **your** problem? Write some."*

—Peggy Shaw,
in conversation with the author, 1989

Because we are in the process of lampooning the stereotypes of our oppressors, we are aware of stereotypes evolving in our own subculture, and we'll lampoon those as well. The queer theater artists I met were unwilling to further any stereotypes in our community.

From the scripts we keep getting, it seems that lesbian theater is still in the kitchen. We have plays about lesbians eating, lesbians coming out to each other. We want to get beyond that.

—Faith McDevitt, at a panel at the first
International Lesbian and Gay Theater
Conference and Festival, 1989

If queer theater is nothing else, it *is* a good belly laugh—an irreverence for what is the assumed normal heterosexual pattern of relating. Queer theater steals heteronormative mating rituals and makes them gaudy, or strips them bare, or turns them inside out. Our men seduce their men, and this is embarrassing. Our women seduce their women, and live without their men, and this is unforgivable.

What Makes This Theater Different?

Yesterday's theatrical paeans to lesbian and gay lives become today's embarrassing memories. At a recent Theatre Rhinoceros production of **Boys in the Band**, a man sat outside the theater selling rotten tomatoes for audience members to throw at the actors. Lesbian women picketed the San Francisco lesbian and gay film festival for screening **The Killing of Sister George**. Some folks look at **Tea and Sympathy** as homophobic and out of date. And I'm not sure that Jane Chambers would like it if she knew the hushed and awed tones with which her name is uttered in some circles.

Queer theater is in a continual state of flux, just like the queer sensibility from which it's born. We would do well to respect the queer theater pioneers, artists like Mart Crowley, Lillian Hellman, Jane Chambers, Tennessee Williams, Gertrude Stein, and Oscar Wilde. We need to respect them, but we do not need to hold them up as the yardstick for ourselves or other queer artists.

Rather, we'd do better to measure our theater according to what we need and want our theater to accomplish—for ourselves, our audiences, and for all the people who will be touched by our audiences. In my particular brand of queer theater, I want to challenge people's concepts of gender and identity. I want the very act of my assuming another identity onstage to call into question the identity of each and every audience member. Accordingly, when I attend theater, I want my own rigid notions of identity to be shaken up. With this in mind, I've come up with my personal guidelines for a queer theater.

» I look for a theater with artists who focus on self-discovery; too many actors and directors today look to be discovered.

» I identify with and see the need for a theater with an outsider mentality, which tends to be considerate and inclusive of the excluded. Most mainstream theater I see assumes a centralist position, tending toward elitism.

» I look for theater that provokes, not theater that pacifies.

» I don't like theater that assumes or promotes the idea that any identity is superior to any other, or that any images of the culture are sacred because they belong to those with a superior identity. I get excited by theater that struggles to occupy, redefine, and reshape the sacrosanct images of our culture.

» The realism we're accustomed to in most theater consists of a linear story line or, at best, a series of entwined linear story lines. For me, realism may be layered, intricately woven, and nonlinear.

» I look for theater that focuses on transformation, because I go along for the ride and am myself transformed.

» The richest moments in theater are moments infused with love. It can be love gone sour, love gone awry, or unrequited love. It can be hidden love, obsessive love, or a love destined to destroy nations. Love that is spiritual, love that is carnal, love that is all in the mind. This love can be romantic love, brotherly love, sisterly love, or a combination of all the above love. But of all these loves, the most powerful is unconditional love. Not surprisingly, unconditional love is the most difficult to portray onstage.

» I'm especially tired of watching theater that limits itself to the portrayal of heterosexuality—and heterosexual romance only. I look for theater that portrays open sexuality and a wide range of eroticism.

» The sexual power I have seen portrayed in theater has most often been represented in images of abuse, rape, and sexual violence against women and children. I'm looking to see sexual power portrayed as safe, sane, and consensually sadomasochistic.

» Most theater admits to only two genders. I want to see theater that hasn't stopped counting.

» I like humor and comedy. A lot. Especially slapstick that pokes fun at those in power. But a good deal of slapstick is aimed at disempowered, marginalized peoples. Camp is an empowering alternative—camp is Zen-like in its irreverence for the established order, its nonviolence, and its often dizzying use of paradox.

» I live in the constructs of this culture day after day—I don't need a theater that simply portrays more of the same. I like to see theater that uncovers the rickety framework on which are draped the lies of the dominant culture.

» Theater funded by the war chests of capitalism usually ends up a tool of capitalism, in the position of being yet another commodity. Theater funded by the community it supports can then be a tool by which an alternate community may be forged and/or strengthened. But any funding is dangerous if it ties the theater to the funding agent. At some point, queer theater must break ties with its funding sources and seek new sources of income that won't tie it down.

» There's a debate that continues to rage about some nebulous thing called "quality of work" and about what's "professional theater" and what's art, and what's not, and what's obscenity and what's not. I'm tired of supporting theater that seeks to establish itself amongst the canonized classics of this petrified culture. I'm tired of supporting the canon of classics by which all theater is judged, and by which artistic measure is taken. Quality of work can be measured only in the moment, and by those in attendance at the work itself. Increased attendance at theater brings about higher standards of quality. Textbooks about quality, and critics' comments on quality, do not bring about higher standards, but only encourage a uniformity of standards. I'm looking for a theater that seeks no judgment outside of itself—a theater that constantly accomplishes its own aims, continually making itself obsolete. Eventually, this theater moves aside for the next wave of theater artists. There's no question as to whether or not it is art. Of course it is.

» The final measure of a theater piece is this: Did it connect with the audience? Technical expertise is valuable in that it provides the artist with proven methods of connecting with the audience. If the subject of the piece is loving and true, it will connect with the audience—that's the heritage of the fool, the heritage of our shamanic ancestors.

Queer Theater as a Third Space

This type of theater has emerged variously as theater of the oppressed, theater of the absurd, and revolutionary theater. It's the theater that has always risen up in the face of oppression. It's not always been queer, and it won't remain fixed within the queer subculture. But it seems that people who are marginalized by their sexuality, gender, and/or sex/gender expression are today making major contributions to world theater, and we might as well run with that for as long as we can.

This type of theater could also be called any variation of "Theater of the Third Space," and it would include members of any borderline community or noncommunity; it would include anyone who falls through the cracks of the cultural floorboards; it would include anyone who challenges a cultural binary; it would include anyone who is Other. We could call it Freak Theater, or Other Theater, but I'm for calling it Queer Theater, because we're the ones who have the courage and the sense of humor to be doing it these days. I *like* calling it Queer Theater, because it's nice to have something important with *our* name on it for a change.

Queer Theater is not lesbian and gay theater, just like not all lesbians, gays, and transsexuals are queer. Lesbian and gay theater was, at one time, cutting edge, more for its content than any style, but there's a complacency that lesbian and gay theater seems to be slipping into. The early '90s saw a number of lesbian and gay plays, playwrights, and performers achieve mainstream recognition; that's when the negotiating for assimilation began in earnest. Much of the community's theater followed suit.

Theater that had once signaled the charge out of the closet began again to call up the kitchens and bedrooms of our lives. No longer was this community theater raising questions and implicating people; instead, it concentrated on "empower-ment" and providing "positive role models." Queer Theater is shifting—continuing to thrive, but within the smaller venues, the low-budget spaces like Highways in Santa Monica; P.S. 122 in New York; San Francisco's Josie's Cabaret and Juice Joint, or Red Dora's: The Bearded Lady Café; Patrick Scully's cabaret space in Minneapolis; Real Art Ways in Hartford, Connecticut; The Drill Hall and the Institute of Contemporary Arts in London; and the It's Queer Up North Festival in Manchester. Through these ven-ues, and through the more daring larger spaces like the Walker Art Center in Minneapolis, and through on-campus productions at colleges and universities around the world, Queer Theater is continuing to flourish and evolve.

Step by small step, queer artists are crossing over to reach broader and broader audiences, but many queer artists still hold down part-time jobs in addition to their full-time artistic careers. The economy has begun to dictate not only our venues but also the size of our productions. Solo performers and small companies of actors, dancers, and comedians are touring the world—from Michael Kearns's series of brilliant solo performances focusing on AIDS, to the Five Lesbian Brothers' darkly comic chronicles of the lesbian position in the culture. We're seeing one another's performances, and we're learning from one another what works. Our own patchwork individual identities have come together to form a brilliantly complex mosaic of theater for our day—a the-ater that will, hopefully sooner rather than later, seem passé and reactionary. It takes that kind of diversity of work and workers to maintain a Third Space.

It stands to reason that one day, some stu-dent will be poking around in some old library books. And she'll blow the dust off these books, and there'll be works in there by Split Britches, or Doug Holsclaw, or Holly Hughes, or Leland Moss. And she'll read this stuff and maybe she'll yawn and say, "Yeah, so?" Or maybe there'll be a revival of **The AIDS Show** or **Hidden: A Gender**. And maybe there will be someone sitting outside the theater selling rotten tomatoes in response to such reactionary, homophobic, or transphobic work. And that just means that we as queer theater artists will have done our jobs very well indeed, and the artistic banner will have been passed on to the next and more enlightened generation of transformational artists in the spirit of Charles Ludlam—the spirit of the trickster, the shaman, the mystic performer, the outlaw.

And until that time, my feeling is that today we need, as queer artists, to strengthen our outsider sensibility, keep it fluid enough to be inclusive of other outsider groups, inflammatory enough to challenge and wear down the dominant ideology, and full of enough grace and humor to welcome with a laugh the inevitable challenges to our own rigidity.

Promotional photo for the first tour of Hidden: A Gender.
(left to right) Justin Bond, Sydney Erskine, Kate Bornstein.

hidden: a gender

"... the boys and girls up in marketing have come up with the ultimate marketing strategy. We're not going to sell you any products tonight, no, we're going to sell you gender. And you want to buy it.

"You want to buy gender because you want to relieve the nagging feeling that you're not quite a man, you're not quite a woman."

—Doc Grinder

Doc Grinder (Kate) as "The Girlfriend," and Herman (Sydney Erskine) in the first production of Hidden: A Gender.

15

HIDDEN: A GENDER

a play in two acts

I stated in the first edition of this book that there are very few if any guidelines I can suggest or would require for performing this piece—that vision is ultimately the responsibility of the production company. As a result, I've had the great good fortune to have been surprised by new interpretations from productions around the world.

Hidden: A Gender can be performed by any number of actors, in any number of gender configurations, and with any sort of staging. In this edition, I've included stage directions so that folks reading the play can get an idea of how we staged it originally. It's my hope that anyone producing the play in the future will cross out the stage directions before giving the script to the actors. It would probably be helpful to have a nonbinary or genderqueer person with a good sense of humor involved with the production, perhaps as a consultant.

Production rights for **Hidden: A Gender** are held by the publisher of this book; and they and I would love you to contact them about production information. I would certainly enjoy being in touch with anyone who's producing the piece, and I'm glad to be available to consult for any production of the play. You can write the publisher, or tweet me @katebornstein.

Hidden: A Gender was first commissioned by Theatre Rhinoceros Literary Manager Doug Holsclaw. It was first coproduced by Outlaw Productions and Theatre Rhinoceros in San Francisco, November 1989, on the studio stage of Theatre Rhinoceros, under Artistic Director Ken Dixon.

The cast members were Justin Bond (Herculine et al.), Sydney Erskine (Herman et al.), and Kate Bornstein (Doc Grinder et al.).

The production company was:

Director/Dramaturge	Noreen C. Barnes
Stage Manager	Sherry Anderson
Assistant Stage Manager	Rick Garlinghouse
Technical Director and Stage Manager for the Tour	Cayenne Woods
Sound Designer	Lori Dovi
Choreographer	Drew Todd
Publicist/Graphic Designer	Bobby Tyler
Production Photographer	Jill Posener

HIDDEN: A GENDER

a play in two acts

Act I, Scene 1

The staging is a unit set and should suggest the studio and set of a television talk show program, like that of **Geraldo**, **Sally Jessy**, *or* **Oprah**. *It should also include elements of the nineteenth-century ancestor of today's talk shows—the traveling medicine show.*

There are three main playing areas. Downstage right is the space for the host/barker, Doc Grinder. A stool or podium may be used to suggest Doc's position of authority.

Up center is the space for Herculine/Abel. A period (nineteenth-century French) chair, or bed, and a nightstand would be ideal. Since she/he is an "exhibit," and since we are looking back in time at her/him, the lighting could be softer, or the space could be raised slightly, or set behind a scrim.

Downstage left is the space for Herman/Kate. In the original production, this was marked by a reclining leather chair, Herman's father's chair. Herman is also "on display," but since he is in current time, there is no need for different lighting.

DOC GRINDER

*L.C. Doc Grinder is part twentieth-century television talk show host, and part nineteenth-century medicine sideshow barker. It is never clear whether Doc is a man or a woman, and this ambiguity is never acknowledged by Doc him-/herself. Doc speaks directly to the audience, and the actor playing Doc is encouraged to ad lib in response to any audience comments. The whole idea is to encourage the audience to play their part: the television talk show audience. In the original production of the play, the part of Doc Grinder was played by the playwright. Casting a transsexual actor in the role of Doc is not essential, but it does add a neat twist to the viewing of the piece. Doc's theme song begins—a pop rendition of the **Bahn Frei Polka**, by Eduard Strauss. My idea of Doc is that he/she's a real charmer.*

If possible, Doc should enter through the audience, perhaps shaking hands, and then taking the stage with a bow that expects audience applause.

DOC GRINDER

Good evening, ladies and gentlemen. Thank you very much for coming this evening. Are you ready? I hope you're ready for suicide. I hope you're ready for perversion—for piety—for mutilation. I hope you're ready for scientific anomalies far too wretched to be described in mere words, and I am not talking about prime-time television, ladies and gentlemen. No—I am talking about the subject of tonight's show, and that subject is—Gender Blur!

Hot one. I know. But you look liberal enough. You wouldn't be here tonight if you weren't, am I right? Of course I'm right. We are well-fed, well-educated people. We are creative. We want to write the script called America, and we want the starring roles.

But—we do not want to be confused with the bit players. So—we do not cross clearly defined lines. And what's the most clearly defined line of all? Help me out here. That's right! It's the line marked Girls' Locker Room. Men Only. Ladies' Room. Boys Club—No Girls Allowed. Wimmin's Land—Wimmin Born Wimmin Only. We're looking for a few good men, and you've come a long way, baby. But, baby—don't cross that line. Don't ever cross that line.

Ladies and gentlemen, you will tonight meet people who do cross that line—creatures from a world with which I hope you seldom have any contact. The World of Gender Blur!

Gender Blur! We hate the very idea. We fear its practitioners. We scorn its victims. We are terrified to be touched by the taint of this offensive illness. Gender Blur. Why mention it in public, before men and women of good gender standing, such as yourselves?

Grinder's my name. L.C. Grinder. Doc Grinder. Proud of every moment of my life. Proud to have served humanity, in audience situations just like this and for over twenty-five years, by bringing to light news of every disease known to man, woman, and child, but never before have I mentioned Gender Blur—never before! Why now? Could be the moon. Could be the earth shaking under my feet. Could be it's time.

I'm going to brush aside the temptation to wax dramatic, ladies and gentlemen. Yes, I am. And I'm going to drop right down to the bottom line, and what's the bottom line—help me out here—that's right—it's money! My money. Your money. Legal tender.

Now, the boys and girls up in marketing all know that advertisements and commercials don't sell products. Advertisements and commercials sell what? Sex and gender! That's right! And sex and gender sell what? The products! Very good! Sex, because it's sex. And once you've had great sex, well, you're going to want more. And if you've never had great sex, you'll buy anything hoping to get some.

But gender—that's another can of worms. That's a different kettle of fish. That's another pea in a different pod. Simply put, once you buy gender, you'll buy anything in order to keep it. You'll buy anything.

So—the boys and girls up in marketing have come up with the ultimate marketing strategy. We're not going to sell you any products tonight, no, we're going to sell you gender. And you want to buy it.

You want to buy gender because you want to relieve the nagging feeling that you're not quite a man, you're not quite a woman.

(Going up to a woman in the audience) You want to buy gender because you want to be secure in your gender identity, don't you, sir? Excuse me, I am so sorry, ma'am, but that must happen to you a lot *(to someone else in the audience),* you know what I'm talking about here. And *(to a third audience member)* you—you should not be smiling! Back to the show.

Ladies and gentlemen, you will tonight meet not one, but two pitiful persons of doubtful and dubious gender identity. Their stories will shock you, and will, I am sure, convince you of the need to define, enhance, and defend your own gender identities.

In this portion of the stage, and through the magic of Dramatic License, we shall peer into the past one hundred years ago. We shall travel in time and through space to France in the last half of the nineteenth century. There we will meet a beautiful, pious young schoolgirl named Herculine Barbin. Before your very eyes, the years shall pass as leaves falling from a tree, and you will observe her doubts, her fears, her worst dreams come true. If she were not so twisted, I could love her. A candle shall call forth her image.

Now, in this portion of the stage, a most distasteful character— quite alive, I'm afraid—who will entertain us with stories from his offensive and peculiar life. Mister Herman Amberstone.

I? I'll be back from time to time. Just to check and see how you're doing. And to play the parts of other characters as needed. I shall always appear in this portion of the stage. But hush—I feel the presence of our young French beauty coming to life. Do not interrupt her, or she will disappear.

*Doc leaves the stage through the audience as the lights come
up on Herculine.*

Act I, Scene 2

TWELVE-YEAR-OLD HERCULINE

*Herculine, in the original production, was played by (then) male
actor Justin Bond, who made no attempt at comic drag, but
instead managed a carefully prepared cross-gendered performance. Herculine was written to be performed in a classic fourth-
wall style, including no interaction with the audience. She is on
display and doesn't know it. The scene could open with the sound
of nuns singing in chapel. Herculine enters carrying a lit candle.
The sound of the nuns singing fades under her opening lines.*

. . . Holy Mary, Mother of God, pray for us sinners now and at
the hour of our death. Amen. Oh, but Blessed Mother, I am so
happy to be alive today. It's my twelfth birthday! Please don't let
this be the hour of my death. Thank you. Amen. And now, I need
to speak with you, Holy Mother. Don't think this bad, for I absolutely adore the day. I adore the school, and my classmates, and
the Sisters. And I so look forward to becoming sensible, charming, literate, and happy the way the Sisters have promised. Sister
Eleonore has told me that the road to being sensible, charming,
literate, and happy is marked by obedience. And I want to obey
those who know better than me, Blessed Mother—it just seems
at times that all—all know better than me. It gets rather difficult.

That's not why I need to talk with you. Last night, I slipped
out of my dormitory again to visit Lea. I was so quiet no one
knew I was leaving. The bedtime prayer had been said and Sister
Eleonore was not in sight. I took up at random the first object
at hand as I left my room—a little ivory crucifix of very pretty

workmanship—you know the one, Holy Mother. I went without a sound to the room I knew to be Lea's. I held my breath and I bent toward her bed and I kissed her several times. I slipped around her neck—her white, soft, beautiful neck—the crucifix. And I said to her, "Here, my friend, accept this and wear it for me." Her beautiful blond head came up toward me, and she thanked me with a kiss that was full of warmth. Oh, Mother of God, I do hope you are still praying for me.

I had no sooner finished than I started—hastily—to go back the way I had come. Oh, Blessed Mother, I had not gone halfway when familiar footsteps made me tremble. My teacher was behind me and she had seen me. And so, Blessed Mother, I've just come from the office of the Mother Superior—you know how fond I am of her—where she told me she had almost struck me from the list of those to take First Communion this year. I began to weep. She motioned me toward her and she stroked my hair, forgiving me. Oh, Holy Mary—I left Mother Gabrielle with my heart penetrated by the sweetest joy and the deepest gratitude.

I believe that I read too much. I know I am to be innocent, but I have a passion for knowledge that I am told only boys may have. Nurse has told me that—"unremitting study might unsex young girls." But I continue to read. Is this disobedience, Mother Mary? Oh, please give me an answer.

As the lights fade on Herculine's part of the stage and come up on Herman's, the voices of the nuns singing in chapel are heard again.

Hail Mary, full of grace, the Lord is with thee. Blessed art thou among women and blessed is the fruit of thy womb, Jesus. Holy Mary, Mother of God, pray for us sinners now and at the hour of our death. Amen. Only, please don't let this be the hour of my death.

She exits, leaving on stage the burning candle.

Act I, Scene 3

HERMAN

In the original production, Herman was played by female actor Sydney Erskine. As in the case of Herculine, no attempt at masquerading at another gender was made—instead, a more ambiguous gender portrayal was stressed. He's a man who's studied how to be male all his life, but for whom maleness remains foreign. Herman is written to speak directly to the audience, in a Brechtian confrontational manner, but he does not have the freedom to interact with the audience, like Doc. After all, Herman is an exhibit, a freak, a guest on a talk show. Doc is in control.

Herman enters, somewhat self-conscious about appearing before the audience, but it soon becomes evident that he has done this before and is quite adept at speaking to large numbers of people.

This is my father's chair. One of the first rules I remember learning was that no girls were allowed in this chair. Or if they did sit here, they had to pay a quarter. When I was older, and I brought different girlfriends to my parents' house for a visit, I remember I would wait 'til my mother and father had both gone upstairs, and then I'd sit in this chair with my girlfriend and we'd make out, and maybe we'd even have sex on the warm, red leather. And I'd always leave a quarter on the cushion before I'd go up to bed with my girlfriend.

Sounds of children playing in a playground.

I'm four and a half years old, my first day of nursery school. It's the first social experience of my life outside of my family. These are the days when the boys and girls have to play separately—so I start to go off with the other little girls to play. And this teacher—I don't know her name, but I call her Miss Tissue, because she always has a tissue in her sleeve—Miss Tissue says, No No Dear, this is the line for the little girls. And I say, I know, I'm a little girl. And you know the look that grown-ups can give you—the one that says you are loathsome and sick and vile and about to be abandoned. She gives me that look. And I know I'll have to pretend to be a little boy from then on.

(Chanting) Baruch atah adonai, elohanu, melech . . . I'm studying for my Bar Mitzvah! I just know the day I become thirteen, I'm going to become a man. I never really believed that, but I'm hoping the ceremony's going to do its job. On the way to Hebrew School, I pass this deli that has the *National Enquirer* in the window—you know, stuff like "Parents Boil Baby and Eat It." This one week, there's this beautiful blond lady on the cover—and a huge headline that says "SHE WAS A HE." My heart stops. I try to read the article through the store window, but it begins on page three, and I know if anyone sees me staring at the paper the way I am, they'll know I'm a girl, and the jig'll be up. I pass this paper four school days in a row. I know that next week it'll be gone. Friday afternoon, I go in and buy the paper—I never had before, so I know the people in the store know I'm weird just like the beautiful blond lady on the cover. It's Christine Jorgensen. "Ex-GI, Now a Blonde Bombshell." "Look out, guys, that blonde cutie you're dating might have been one of Uncle Sam's finest men!" And then a quote from her— "I'm happy to have become a woman and I think more people who are as unhappy as I was before should follow my example." I read that article over and over and over for a week. Then I burn it.

It wouldn't be for another thirty years that I'd read about Herculine Barbin and fall in love with her. But, back to the story.

It was in eighth grade English class when I learned more than I ever wanted to learn about gender. My teacher was Mr. Blunt. Good afternoon, Mr. Blunt.

Act I, Scene 4

MR. BLUNT

In the original production, Blunt was played by Doc Grinder in semi–clown getup. He's a weary nerd of a high school English teacher. Because he's played by Doc, he addresses the audience directly, as though they are an unruly class of high school students, and he interacts with them accordingly.

Herman. Good afternoon, class. Today's lesson involves pronouns and gender. It is very important to use the correct pronoun to refer to the correct person—stop the snickering in the back row—all right, I'm only going to say this once, so you'd better take notes. I'm not going to repeat myself. Pronouns and gender. I has no gender. Neither does you.

He and she definitely have a specific gender which is very helpful to all of—us—because we doesn't have a gender either. Does we?

Back to he and she or rather to him and to her. He is masculine except when he is universal and means him and her and all of—us, who has no gender still.

She is feminine, except of course when she is inanimate, like a ship or a salad, but six of one, half a dozen of the other, am I right?

We still doesn't have a gender. You plural has no gender either.

Unlike him and her, they has no gender whatsoever, which I will admit introduces some confusion, but we're almost finished so live with it.

It has no gender at all, except of course when it refers to an infant about whose gender we are uncertain. Not unlike me. Or you.

There will be a quiz next Tuesday.

A buzzer sounds, indicating the end of the class. Herman and Blunt exit.

Act I, Scene 5

SEVENTEEN-YEAR-OLD HERCULINE

Enters running. In the original production, Herculine played this scene to an imaginary "Grandpappa."

Grandpappa! Grandpappa! Poppy, you've a letter from Paris, from your sister! Shall I read it to you? Yes, of course I shall. Sit, while I light another candle. I don't know why you so love dark corners. Here now—

"My Dearest Baptistin, I know it's been ages since I've written you, so my warmest greetings to you, dear Brother. And to you, sweet Herculine . . ."

She's writing to me too!

". . . I know you are reading this to my crusty old brother. Your ghoulish grandfather adores sitting in the darkest corners of his house, so go, girl, and light another candle . . ."

Aunt Carmilla knows us each so well, Poppy—one would think she could read minds!

". . . Very well then. Today, I was accused, in all sincerity, and by an otherwise sober gentleman, of being a vampire. Paris is going mad! I moved here twenty years ago because the Parisians celebrated artists and courtesans. Alas—now they call us vampires. Truly. Vampires are all the rage now . . ."

That's true—but the sisters will not permit us to speak of vampires.

". . . From what I can piece together, loose women such as I are vampires because we . . ."

Loose women such as . . . ?

". . . loose women such as I are vampires because we desire the essence of men's fluids, and will stop at nothing to procure these precious fluids. Piffle. I've not been interested in a single man since Henri died, and that was over fifteen years ago.

Babette and I have quite a comfortable arrangement, thank you very much. She is more of a woman than the frivolous coquettes who parade the Left Bank, and, I confess, more of a man than my sweet departed Henri . . ."

I—I know more than a few unusual girls like this in convent school.

". . . Oh, poor Herculine, I am so sorry if I shock you, but according to my calculations, you are now seventeen years old . . ."

Seventeen years and five months, thank you.

". . . and it's about time you heard about life in Paris . . ."

As if I didn't know about life in Paris!

". . . Do come visit me, Herculine, and we can be vampires together! They say now that we women are creatures of darkness—that we belong only to the night, the moon, and the stars, Herculine. Brother dearest—you men, of course, have inherited the sun, the warmth, and the day. Ha! . . ."

Ha? Oh—"Ha!"

". . . The irony is that I dare not go out in the street at night for fear of personal injury. It's true there are no men out at night. Only beasts. If I am a vampire, then they are the werewolves . . ."

She must be speaking in metaphors. Yes. She is.

". . . Speaking of blood—my anemia is much improved. I stop round the slaughterhouse with other blood-drinkers for my daily cup of ox blood, and that seems to help. Perhaps this medicine only further shows I am a vampire? Dear Brother, I am enclosing for your pleasure Rachilde's latest novel, *Mister Venus*. It's a delightful story of a woman who keeps a man as her male mistress in an apartment . . ."

. . . male mistress?

". . . watching him grow fat and slothful and passive in response to her possessive behavior . . ."

This is rubbish, Grandpappa. Still, I suppose it is readable.

". . . Herculine, promise me you will become no man's mistress. I must run, my dears, the moon is rising, and I feel the urge to bite the neck of my sweet Babette . . ."

If she insists on doing these perversities with another woman, why does she insist on talking about them, and why to me? Why to me? She . . .

". . . Your loving sister and aunt, Carmilla."

Vampires and artists, really! Grandpappa—Poppy, do you think someone, anyone, would go to Hell for doing what Aunt Carmilla is doing with Miss Babette?

Blackout. The candles remain burning, and Herculine exits.

Act I, Scene 6

HERMAN

Herman enters, picking up the book from Herculine's night-stand and, thumbing through it, he walks over to his area stage left.

I'd read anything I could get my hands on. Anything that would tell me what I was. Who I was. What gender I was.

Herculine learned about being a woman from the nuns, and from her aunt, the vampire. I watched television. I read *Life* magazine. I began to study acting. With each man's part I played, I learned more about how men were supposed to . . . act.

I was a good actor. In the late sixties, I played this motorcycle tough guy who could get all the women he wanted. I had no idea where to start and so my director had to coach me on how to move, how to talk, what to wear.

And I wore these dark glasses and I wore this leather jacket. I was in real bad-boy drag. I even grew my sideburns yes I did. Bad boy. And my director he taught me how to walk—not like that, he'd say as I'd saunter across the stage. Not like that, you lead with your pelvis. Walk this way, he'd say, it's a pelvic thrust. And together we'd walk around the stage. And it was dark on that stage, with just a few rehearsal lights on, and I had these dark glasses and I couldn't see and walk this way he'd say and I'd let my penis do the walking, and I just went along for the ride, taking notes.

And I had lines like, "Women are not individuals, but types. No, not even types, just women. They want to surrender, but they don't want the responsibility of surrendering." And I thought to myself, yeah? Is that it? And I'd walk my walk, and I'd talk my talk and I learned how to get women. Yes I did. I learned to do whatever I had to do in order to get women. And I learned that once I got her, she'd do anything. I learned. And I walked this way, and the women lined up.

Enter The Girlfriend, played by Doc Grinder **en femme**. *The Girlfriend sits down on the stool in Doc's space.*

They just lined up outside my dressing room door. They wanted that stud. And I learned to be that stud. They wanted the leather jacket and they wanted the eyes they couldn't see and I wanted them so that's who I became. I wanted every one of those women. And one by one I fucked them and they fucked the character they'd just seen onstage. I fucked them over.

THE GIRLFRIEND
And despite all of that, he was still a sensitive kind of guy.

HERMAN
Trust me . . .

THE GIRLFRIEND
. . . he'd say to me . . .

HERMAN

. . . I understand you. Trust me . . .

THE GIRLFRIEND

. . . he'd say . . .

HERMAN

. . . I need you. Trust me . . .

THE GIRLFRIEND

. . . he said . . .

HERMAN

. . . I love you. I really love you.

THE GIRLFRIEND

How could you not fall for a guy like that?

HERMAN

And every night the lines outside the stage door got longer and every woman on that line convinced me I was a man. I learned. I was that stud. I learned. I had the Marlboro Man by the balls and I could fuck like the best of the boys. I learned. So I couldn't be a woman. Not if I loved women so much. I learned. How could I be a woman? How could I?

Act I, Scene 7

DOC GRINDER

*Doc is still **en femme**. Before this scene, Doc was a hard-boiled male talk show host. Now he's a more sympathetic **female** talk show host. Doc neither acknowledges nor makes any*

*concession to this change in gender, which isn't exaggerated at
all, but which is very different from his male persona.*

Yes, strange as it seems, he still feels like a woman. It's gender
blur. We don't think about our gender day and night. Not like
these poor victims. No, it doesn't even cross our mind. No. Not
until someone calls you sir again. Not until someone says you're
behaving too effeminately. Experts agree that we don't even think
about gender in terms of ourselves. No, it's not until we see
someone walking down the street and we can't tell if it's a man
or a woman. Ever wonder why you can't stop staring until you
decide one way or the other? It really bothers you, doesn't it!

We don't have to know someone's age. Their race may be
somewhat indistinct, and we might be mildly curious. We may
look at someone and think are they gay or straight, but we don't
have to know. We can wonder. Yet we insist, and this is the curi-
osity, we insist that a person be one gender or the other and we
remain unsettled until we assign one gender or the other. It's part
of our conscience, isn't it?

And, as to conscience—we really should thank religion, whose
chief task, it seems to be, is to see that we all have more or less the
exact same conscience.

*Herman comes up behind Doc, pushing his hips into Doc's
backside.*

My rod and my staff shall comfort me.

Herman and Doc tango off together.

Act I, Scene 8

HERCULINE

The tango music continues. Herculine enters and stands facing
the audience as though she is examining herself in a mirror. We
can see by the way she is touching herself and looking that she
is naked. She observes her breasts, muscles, cunt, long clitoris,
beard. She is distraught and enters a confessional. In the original
production, this was done by Herculine walking to a small stool,
kneeling on it, and speaking as if through a confessional window.

Forgive me Father for I have sinned. I fear I am becoming a vampire. My aunt is a vampire and she wrote me what it means to be
one. My passion for God is at war with my passion for my studies.
I am reading at every opportunity. And with every bit of knowledge I gain, I lose more and more of my innocence. I am falling
away from all that is womanly. I am not interested in mother-
hood. I am not the least bit interested in arts and crafts. Two men
have proposed marriage to me, and my response is revulsion.
I . . . I am . . . My body—my body is changing.

Father, I do not yet desire blood, as does a true vampire, but
I do desire a vampire's natural prey, namely other women. I have
lustful thoughts and intentions for Therese, a student in my dormitory. We have kissed several times, and I take every opportunity I can to be near her, and to feel her so warm near me. I am
frustrated with my own timidity, and at times I wish to play the
part of a man with her. Oh, Father, I fear I am turning into a man.
Listen to me. I know that carnal deeds are harmful and sinful.
Why do I hunger so for Therese? How can I have a woman's passion for life and a man's thirst for knowledge? How can I have a
woman's yearning for peace with my God, and a man's lust for
women? What am I, Father?

My sins? Three nights ago, it was during the storm. I had sto-
len to the bedside of my Therese. I was stroking her hair, inhaling

her scent, listening so carefully to her breath, her sighs. And then the terrible stroke of lightning and that awful clap of thunder. Father, I felt the hand of Our Lord pushing me away from her side. And I fought that. I clasped her to me, and though the wind howled and the nuns raised their voices in prayer, I held Therese and she held me. And with each peal of thunder we kissed so deeply and breathed our fear and exultation into each other's mouths until, until we were both—exhausted.

If I am becoming a vampire, or if I am becoming a man then I know I am falling away from God. Father—what am I?

Blackout. Herculine exits.

Act I, Scene 9

HERMAN

Enters and sits in his chair.

I'd pray. I'd pray each night to wake up and be a woman. I'd pray in detail. Details like the taste and scent of every woman I'd slept with. Not their names. I was too stoned for their names. Details like going to sleep nights—sometimes alone, mostly not—but every night praying to God that I'd wake up and be a woman and every morning I'd wake up with a hand on my cock, sometimes my hand—mostly someone else's—god they loved my cock and I never had the courage to say you do? you really do? well, hey then—take it, have it. Put it on the wall over your bed, just get it away from me. And it wasn't the cock so much as what the cock had me trapped in. I thought to myself, girl, you are one evil son of a bitch. You are one sick puppy. You had better crawl back into the hole you've been trying to dig yourself out of yes sir, girl.

And one day in Boston, Massachusetts, the lights went on. These big old 400-watt lamps went on in my brain and lit up corners of my mind I wished I swept up years before. I needed to find the answers to the world's problems, not mine! So I quit graduate school and got into my VW camper with my *I Ching* and my Tarot cards and my miso and my sprouts and I went off to Denver to climb a mountain and come down with the answer to the world's problems.

I needed hiking boots so I could climb the mountain. The store was closed, and next door there was this poster of an old monk in a cave, holding up a torch and looking into an open treasure chest. And the poster said, "Abandon Your Tedious Search— The Answers Have Been Found." And I thought—far out—what is this Church of Scientology anyway?

And I went in and these folks were eating pizza, and I thought— wow—enlightened and eating pizza! I read their books and they were onto me. Whole sections about perverts like me and how sick we were. Homoseckshuls, lesbins, rapists, psychiatrists, and politicians. And I thought—far out—if they can see how sick and twisted I am, then this is the group for me! Six years later, I'm their leading spokesman in Europe and the Eastern United States. I'd give these lectures. I'd sell immortality.

And they'd spend $250 an hour to get it. I'd sell this stuff thinking this is my spiritual penance, man, this is what I need to do so next lifetime I can be born a woman.

Hey—everyone wants immortality. It's a surefire sale. You want it, don't you? Oh, I don't mean in the same body—you'd have the ability to choose your own parents next time around. Neat, huh? You can get started for only $25,000. And they wrote the checks—they just kept writing those checks. I gave 'em a show.

One day, I'm in the Scientology sales office in New York and this woman walks into my office and says she needs to see me. I ask her to sit down and she does and she's crying. Only she's going boo-hoo-hoo, just like that. Boo-hoo-hoo, boo-hoo, boo-hoo-hoo. Nobody really cries like that. And some of the other sales reps who knew her were standing in the doorway behind her and they were laughing real quiet so she couldn't hear. They were just bustin' a gut shakin' like jelly turnin' all red and she's going boo-hoo, boo-hoo-hoo. And it turns out she's a transsexual and she's had this operation to make her a woman and now that she's gotten into Scientology they've convinced her she's done the wrong thing and she wants to know if she pays enough money to me can she grow another cock and the guys in the doorway they just keep on laughing and I have to tell her I don't know if you can grow another cock. I don't know what I can do for you. I just don't know.

DOC GRINDER

Enters through the audience, taking the stage on his stool. He has both male and female elements.

I thought we cut that bit.

HERMAN

I, uh . . . left the Church of Scientology some years later when I found out that all the money I'd been making was going into the Swiss bank accounts of the founder. And I was free to explore my—my gender blur. I started asking questions.

Act I, Scene 10

DOC GRINDER

Questions. Queries, conundrums, bones of contention. Questions. Quests. Did you ever go on a quest to discover your gender identity? You never had to sort that out, did you? Of course not. None of us do.

Some of you should.

But, let us return in time. Our beautiful nineteenth-century heroine has graduated and has obtained a teaching position in a private school for girls. Two years have passed. Herculine is once again carrying on—having an affair with another woman. This time it's Sara—the daughter of the headmistress. That is, until the night the pains began for Herculine, and a doctor had to be called in. It seems the good doctor found the source of Herculine's pains to be a pair of healthy testicles descending into her labia. Her otherwise perfectly formed vagina opened into no uterus. It was a dead end. Her clitoris was found to be an intriguing two inches long. *(To an audience member)* Now—how did I know *you'd* like that part?

Bear witness now to what the doctor found. And the questions. Queries, conundrums, bones of contention. Questions.

Blackout. Doc and Herman exit in the darkness.

Act I, Scene 11

HERCULINE

A single pin spot illuminates only her face.

Why is he asking me all these questions! Oh-h-h-h-h-h what is causing me this pain? When did I last have my menstrual flux? Ha! I never have, and that's—ow-w-w-w-w-w please may I have some more laudanum?

No man has seen me like he is seeing me now. I want his hands to stop touching ow-w-w-w-w-w! I wish Sara were here to hold my hand no I don't. No I don't. When does the laudanum begin to ease the pain, doctor? What does he mean by descending? Sara, he won't stop—is it because I have loved you? I love you.

Testicles? Have I ever . . . with how many men? None! What is he speaking about—draining their semen their fluids in the night. What? I grow somewhat light-headed. The laudanum of course of course of course I am a vampire. No—only women. Suck? Yes, of course. Ow-w-w-w-w-w!

Doctor, I have had no men in my life but the priests, my grandfather, and now yourself. I've—what's in that jar? One? One what? Two? What are those . . . GET THOSE LEECHES AWAY FROM ME! PLEASE! PLEASE! Don't! Please don't. Not up inside me! Oh no, no, no, no, no. My head is too cloudy. Three? Four! Four leeches up inside me am I losing my mind? He has counted them aloud saying he wishes not to lose any. Leeching a vampire! Hail Mary full of grace the Lord is with thee blessed are thou among women and blessed is the fruit of thy womb oh Jesus I feel them moving inside me Holy Mary mother of God pray for us vampires now and at the hour of our death amen. Please, please let this be that hour!

Has what gotten longer? That? Sara calls that my man part yes you do, my love. Yes. Yes it has since my arrival at the school. I've become a what?

Oh, no—no no no no no I am a woman. I am sensible I am charming I am literate I am happy I am what men are not. Men are busy—I am to be idle. Men are rough—I am to be gentle. Men are strong—I am to be frail. Men are rational—I am . . . I am rational. God help me I must be a man. What? Yes, more laudanum, of course. I have no uterus? What in heaven's name is a uterus? Oh.

Sara, he is saying I am a man. He is saying I am a man and I must obey him for I am nothing if I am not obedient. Why is my head spinning? Sara—two women cannot be lovers. It is obscene.

Four leeches are growing fat on the last traces of my womanhood and shortly I will be nothing but a man. I am a man. I have questions, doctor. I do not question you. I have questions. I am a man. A man can question things, can he not?

Blackout.

Act I, Scene 12

DON'S VOICE

*In the original production, this prerecorded talk played in the
blackness and was performed by the same actor who plays
Herculine.*

Questions? Did somebody say questions? That can mean only one
thing!

Drumroll.

Ladies and gentlemen, joining us tonight is our current champion. Over thirty years of successfully answering questions and
tonight is the final night—the night for the grand prize—ladies
and gentlemen, welcome our returning champ, Herman Amberstone, to the grand finale round of *What's My Gender!*

*Canned applause, music. The lights come up to reveal a very
puzzled and nervous Herman seated on a stool center stage.
The voice-over continues.*

What's My Gender!—the fun question and answer game brought
to you by Doc Grinder's famous elixir, Gender Defender, in the
pink and blue bottles. And now for our Master, or is it Mistress, of
Ceremonies—L.C. Doc Grinder!

DOC GRINDER

*Doc enters as the male game show host. The audience be-
comes a game show audience.*

Thank you, Don, thank you, and hi there, folks! Well, Herman,
you're a champ at this, but I'm going to review the rules for our

studio audience. We're going to be asking Herman some very intimate questions—anything and everything about his, or is it her, gender identity. There are no right answers, but our champ has to answer these questions to his, or is it her, own satisfaction. Are you ready, Herman?

HERMAN

Yes, L.C., I am.

DOC GRINDER

All right! Then, let's play round one of . . . *What's My Gender!*

Your first question—Herman, you may think you're a woman—aren't you really just a gay man who's so afraid of being gay that the only way to have sex with men is to be a woman?

Canned audience reaction—ooooooooo.

HERMAN

No—no, L.C., I've thought about that one a lot—I don't want sex with men. Tried it a few times to make sure . . .

DOC GRINDER

I'll bet he did!

HERMAN

. . . and I'm not cut out for that. So—I'm not a gay man.

Canned audience—aw-w-w-w-w-w.

DOC GRINDER

Hey—he's not a gay man! But that's just the first of our questions. The next question is . . . oh, this is a killer . . . Herman, can't you just dress up like a woman, occasionally, like a hobby?

Canned audience reaction—whoa-oa-oa.

HERMAN

It's not the clothes, L.C.—I feel I'm a woman no matter what I'm wearing.

Canned audience reaction—mmmmmmmmmmmmmm.

DOC GRINDER

Works for me. Tell you what, folks—let's take a short commercial break while we try to figure out his answer to that last question, and then we'll return to play . . . *What's My Gender!*

DON'S VOICE

What's My Gender! is brought to you by Doc Grinder's Gender Defender, the miracle elixir that keeps you straight. In the pink bottles for girls, and the blue bottles for men. And now—back to our show!

DOC GRINDER

Here we are, ladies and gentlemen—after over thirty years of successfully answering questions, and tonight's the final night! Are you ready, Herman?

HERMAN

As ready as I'll ever be, L.C.

DOC GRINDER

All right, big fellah, good luck to you. And the next question is—do you have any idea of the privileges you'll be giving up that belong only to heterosexual white men, and the limitations you'll face as a woman?

Canned audience—oooooo!

HERMAN

Yes.

DOC GRINDER

That's it? That's your answer. Why, you . . . *(looks offstage)* Well, hey—Hey! Bold move! A totally unjustified answer! And the judges are going to buy it.

Canned audience applause.

Don't get carried away!

Canned audience stops.

Now—the final question before we ask him *What's His Gender!*—*(drumroll)* Herman, how can you be a woman if you love women sexually and romantically?

Canned audience—assorted gasps.

HERMAN

My gender identity has nothing to do with my sexual preference. Gender identity for me answers the question of who I am. Sexual preference answers the question who do I want to be romantically or sexually involved with. My being a woman does not mean I must love men. These are two separate issues.

DOC GRINDER

Two separate issues??!? What are you trying to . . .

Canned wild audience applause. Doc looks offstage to "the judges."

Of course they are. Two separate issues. I knew that one myself. We're going to return to ask him what's his gender, but first— Don, why don't you tell our studio audience what our champion will win . . . if he has the courage to go through with this.

DAWN'S VOICE

Don has become Dawn.

All right, L.C.—Herman has a lot to look forward to! If he or she wins and names his or her gender, then he or she wins one dozen bottles of ice-blue Secret deodorant—strong enough for a man, but gentle enough for a woman. And two dozen pairs of Jockey shorts. Or Jockey for Her, as the case may be. And three dozen pairs of Hanes support socks, or support panty hose—either way, gentlemen prefer Hanes! And last, but not least, Herman will win a lifetime supply of Doc Grinder's Gender Defender, the miracle elixir that keeps you straight. Gender Defender—one bottle and your fears disappear! Two bottles and your family breathes a sigh of relief. Three bottles and you can vote Republican. Back to you, L.C.

DOC GRINDER

Thank you, Dawn—thank you very much. And now—it's time for the final question. The killer conundrum, the bone of contention. Herman Amberstone—for all those great products, and for a year's supply of Doc Grinder's Gender Defender, my miracle elixir that keeps you straight, in the pink bottles for the girls, and the blue bottles for the men—Herman, What's Your Gender?

From the audience come canned shouts of "Man, go for man!" or "Woman, be a woman!"

HERMAN

I'm a woman.

Doc laughs, snaps his fingers, signaling triumphant music, confetti, wild applause, cheers. Blackout.

Act II, Scene 1

The lights come up on the stage, catching by surprise the First Actor, played by "Herman," and the Second Actor, played by "Herculine." They are carrying a bucket, dustpan, and broom, sweeping up something from everywhere. Doc enters, unaware of the presence of the other two, and begins to speak.

DOC GRINDER

Given the luxury of self-examination . . .

FIRST ACTOR

DON'T MOVE TO YOUR LEFT!!!

DOC GRINDER

WHAT!!?!!

FIRST ACTOR

Sorry, you almost stepped in some.

DOC GRINDER

Thank you, I . . . almost stepped in *what*?

FIRST ACTOR

Gender—it's all over the place. Careful!

DOC GRINDER

Oh, well, I see, I . . . Wait a minute! Are you telling me you're sweeping up . . . gender?!!

FIRST ACTOR

Yep, bucket's almost full. We lose a lot during the first act.

SECOND ACTOR

Tons. Just tons.

DOC GRINDER

And so there's gender all over the stage? *(Sitting)* I don't see any!

SECOND ACTOR

Well, I'm not the least bit surprised—you're sitting in some.

DOC GRINDER

The gender on Doc's stool pokes and prods at Doc, who is trying valiantly to remain seated. One final shove from the gender, though, and he's tossed off onto the stage. The Second Actor cleans off a final bit of gender from the stool with a flourish.

Listen you—I've got one more monologue, and then you're on. Hadn't you better get ready?

SECOND ACTOR

To First Actor, ignoring Doc.

We have enough?

FIRST ACTOR

I think so—go ahead—I'll bring this back to the dressing room.

SECOND ACTOR

Bye, girls!

DOC GRINDER

(To Second Actor) You! Put that down, and get over here! Do you mean to tell me you do this every night?

FIRST ACTOR

Yeah, we usually do it during intermission, but tonight's a better audience, so there's a whole lot more—they lose some, we lose some—it adds up.

DOC GRINDER

Well, that makes sense, I . . . GET BACK OVER HERE! You mean everyone's gender is mixed up in there?

FIRST ACTOR

Yeah, so?

DOC GRINDER

There's male and female mixed up in here?

FIRST ACTOR

Oh! You think male and female is gender!

Music under: honky-tonk version of **The Stars and Stripes Forever.**

Nah, that's not gender. Gender is the feeling that you need to be one or the other. Gender is the need to belong—it doesn't matter to what. Gender is the need to fit in, be part of something. All the rest is marketing. Sales. Public Relations.

DOC GRINDER

Well, sure, then . . . GIVE ME THAT!

Doc pulls the bucket from First Actor, falling and spilling its contents onto an audience member in the first row. The gender is loose in the studio! He nervously approaches the audience member.

Do you feel any different? No? No! Of course not! Ha! Now *(to First Actor)*—don't you have some acting to do?!!!

FIRST ACTOR

Is this acting? Is this dialogue?

STAGE MANAGER'S VOICE

Hey, you guys—five minutes to the Marx Brothers bit.

FIRST ACTOR

Gotta run. You're so cute when you're angry.

First Actor exits.

DOC GRINDER

Yes, well. Ladies and gentlemen—forgive the interruption—this evening's entertainment is being brought to you by Doc Grinder's Gender Defender. The medicine so strong you don't even need to take it in order for it to work. One look at the bottle and you know what you are. In the pink bottle for the girls and the blue bottle for the men.

But, my Gender Defender is only the latest in a long line of medical accomplishments in the field of Gender. Let us return to our two misfits, and see how their doctors cared for them.

Oh—you do know what "care" is, don't you? Care is a curious

and efficient blend of love and hate—with none of the messiness of commitment and responsibility. As in under your doctor's care. As in I care about you. Deeply.

Act II, Scene 2

HERCULINE

Herculine enters, dressed awkwardly as a man, and speaks to an imaginary sleeping Sara.

Sara? Sara, are you awake? Of course you're not. The doctor said those powders would cause you to sleep 'til noon tomorrow. It was the only way I could leave you, dearest. I know you don't want me as a man, and I must leave for Paris to begin my life as one. I must obey the doctor.

Oh, sweet love, I hope you will one day come to see, as I have seen, why I must do this. According to Dr. Tardieu, I am a man chiefly because I cannot bear children. The mysterious uterus is present nowhere in my body. According to the doctor, it was all the reading I did as a child that caused my uterus to vanish and my, um, man part to begin to grow. The good doctor agreed with Father Michael that too much knowledge is incompatible with the innocence which is women's nature. It's why I've loved women so intensely, and we both know how unnatural it is for two women to love one another as we have done. The doctor went on to say that while he heard I was an excellent teacher, that was simply further proof that my nervous system had indeed become male. He's really quite taken with my state of affairs—he says I am evolving from a lower life-form to a higher one. That I shall soon be able to enjoy power, knowledge, and more women than I could ever imagine. Once my man-part grows in. He said I must practice my manhood rigorously, for androgynous character is often accompanied by imbecility, and he caught me just in time before my mind began to deteriorate. He said I've lived my life as a pencil sketch, and to prepare for a life as rich and as full as an oil painting.

You know I've never been quite happy with my lot, Sara. Perhaps I shall find happiness as a man. I am terrified. I know nothing of men, and I've been discontented with my life as a woman. I confess to a thrill at fulfilling a vast desire for the unknown. Sara, I am too full of excitement and too full of myself to regret the very dear ties I am breaking now of my own free will.

Sara—the doctor has laid such temptations at my door! He said that women, and other lower forms of humans, like the blackamoors and the Orientals—that these lower forms of life are valued for, oh what did he say, they are valued for loyalty, intimacy, hard physical work, obedience, devotion, and their ability to serve and nurture men. Us. Me.

Can you see this is my escape? Can you see this is my freedom? Sara, I was never meant to be some man's wife or indeed the serving maid of anyone. Before this door to manhood opened, I had no path but the path of virtual slavery—or persecution as some vampire—for that is woman's lot. I only wish I had the courage to say this to you while you were awake. I was never brave. I'm sure that will come with time, and perhaps I shall visit you and . . . no. That will never be. I could never face you again. That part of me shall always remain coward.

Sara—we yielded to each other's love. What will it be like to fulfill my destiny as a man by conquering women? Dominating their desires? For all this has the doctor promised me. Good-bye my sweetest love. Forgive me one day. Good-bye.

Herculine exits.

Act II, Scene 3

HERMAN

Herman enters, dressed androgynously, and addresses the audience.

I'm transsexual, I said to my wife.
I'm not a lesbian, she said, good-bye.
I'm transsexual, I said to my friends.
We don't know you, they said, good-bye.
I'm transsexual, I said to my mother.
You're my child, she said, but for now good-bye.
I'm transsexual, I said to my boss.
Can you still sell, he said, get back to work.
I'll need time to go to the hospital, I said to him.
Good-bye, he said.
I'm definitely transsexual, I said to my first shrink.
I wonder, he said, how our therapeutic relationship would
    change,
he said, if he were to leave his home and his wife and his two
children, he said, and we were to shack up together, he said.
Good-bye, I said.
I'm transsexual, I said to the surgeon's nurse on the phone,
and I'd like an appointment.
Two o'clock next Friday, she said, good-bye.

Herman exits.

Act II, Scene 4

This scene is done in the style and character of a Marx Brothers skit. Doc is Dr. Razor, the Groucho figure. The actor playing

Herculine plays both Nurse Dimple, a Marx Brothers dumb blonde, and Dr. Weener, a Harpo character. Herman plays the straight man.

NURSE DIMPLE

Two o'clock next Friday, good-bye. Razor and Weener, general surgeons, hello. No, Dr. Razor and Dr. Weener aren't in right now. They're in surgery. I expect them any moment. I'll be sure to tell them. Good-bye. Oh, good morning, Dr. Razor!

DR. RAZOR

Doc Grinder enters as Dr. Razor, wearing a white lab coat. Instead of a cigar, he twirls a vibrator in his hand.

Never mind that, Nurse Dimple, get the hospital on the phone! Get the surgeon general on the phone! I just finished a sex-change operation, changing a man to a woman, and I made a terrible mistake!

NURSE DIMPLE

Oooooo, doctor, whatever happened?

DR. RAZOR

I forgot to remove half the patient's brain!

Nurse Dimple laughs hysterically.

You know, I can never tell if she's laughing or if she's choking. Of course, that's the way it is with *all* my women.

NURSE DIMPLE

Dr. Razor! You have a message to call Frank's Fresh Fish and Bait.

DR. RAZOR

Frank's Fresh Fish and Bait? What do they want, nurse?

NURSE DIMPLE

They want their money, doctor.

DR. RAZOR

And exactly how much do we owe them, nurse?

NURSE DIMPLE

You owe them nine thousand dollars, doctor.

DR. RAZOR

Egad! That's the most expensive and delicate part of the whole
sex-change procedure!

NURSE DIMPLE

What's that, doctor?

DR. RAZOR

Sewing in the day-old fish!

*He pulls a dead fish from his pocket, tossing it aside. Nurse
Dimple chokes.*

She's definitely choking now!

NURSE DIMPLE

Dr. Razor, they're not the only creditors calling! Bill collectors
have been calling all morning! They say they're tired of phoning
and something will have to be done!

DR. RAZOR

Okay, we'll do something, nurse—marry me, and we'll move to the next state!

NURSE DIMPLE

Oooooo, doctor!

DR. RAZOR

But seriously, nurse, we need a new patient with lots of money.

NURSE DIMPLE

Well, you have a Herman Amberstone coming in at two today—that's any minute from now, doctor.

DR. RAZOR

Amberstone, Amberstone—hey, sounds Jewish to me!

HERMAN

Hello, you must be Dr. Razor.

They do a handshake bit, ending up with Dr. Razor slapping the vibrator into Herman's outstretched hand. The vibrator goes off, falling to the floor, buzzing away. Doc retrieves it from the floor, turning it off.

HERMAN

A good friend of mine told me you're an excellent sex-change surgeon.

NURSE DIMPLE

Ooooh, honey—you just *think* that's a good friend of yours.

DR. RAZOR

Nurse Dimple, I'll handle the punch lines around here. Unless of course, you'd like a punch yourself!

Nurse Dimple exits, Dr. Razor follows her out, admiring her swaying derriere, but at the last minute turns back to Herman.

Now, young fellow, what can I do for you?

HERMAN

Well, I'm here about a sex change.

DR. RAZOR

Sex change! Why didn't you say so? I know what a sex change is! What is it? Sex of one—half a bosom of the other.

Herman attempts to leave.

Hold on there youngster, I'll call in my associate—Dr. Weener! Oh—DOC-TOR WEE-E-E-ENER!

NURSE DIMPLE *(offstage)*

Dr. Weener! You masher!

Sound of slap, Dr. Weener enters with a rolling pratfall—replete with Harpo wig, white lab coat, and horn.

DR. WEENER

(honk)

DR. RAZOR

Well, hello, Dr. Weener!

DR. WEENER

(honk)

DR. RAZOR

You don't say!

DR. WEENER

(honk, honk)

DR. RAZOR

You don't say!

DR. WEENER

(honk, honk, honk)

DR. RAZOR

You don't say!

HERMAN

What did all that mean?

DR. RAZOR

I don't know, he didn't say! Probably something very technical and very medical about the sex-change procedure we plan to use.

DR. WEENER

Running in circles around Herman, "examining" him lasciviously, while Herman is trying to fend him off with a chair.

(honk)

HERMAN

And what procedure do you plan to use?

DR. RAZOR

Leaning his head on Herman's shoulders, rolling his eyes.

For what, dollface?

HERMAN

To make a new vagina!

DR. WEENER

(honk)

Dr. Weener demonstrates the procedure by pulling a banana from his lab coat, slowly peeling it, then breaking off a large hunk of banana and hurling it offstage. He turns to Herman, triumphantly.

(honk)

HERMAN

That does it. I'm outta here.

He attempts to leave, but is stopped by both doctors.

DR. RAZOR

Hold on there, young fellow. I'll have you know that we—Dr. Razor and Dr. Weener—are the tops in our field. Why, we have diplomas from everywhere!

Both doctors open their lab coats, revealing many important diplomas.

And you won't find a better pair of surgeons in all of Philadelphia!

HERMAN

Oh, all right. You're the boss.

DR. RAZOR

I'm the boss? Well, that's more like it! In that case, get back to work. And you can forget about your promotion.

HERMAN

I'm not getting a promotion?

DR. RAZOR

I should say not! You're becoming a woman, and that's a demotion if I ever heard of one! So tell me, is your boyfriend going to help you out with the money for the surgery?

HERMAN

I don't have a boyfriend.

DR. RAZOR

No boyfriend! Fiancé, then?

HERMAN

I don't have a fiancé.

DR. RAZOR

No fiancé! But you are seeing a man, aren't you?

HERMAN

No.

DR. RAZOR

But you are planning on marrying a man, adopting two-point-three children, a dog, a third of a cat, and a white picket fence?

HERMAN

Sometimes I think about a white picket fence. And I have two cats.

DR. RAZOR

Two cats! Are you telling me you're planning to become a . . . lesbian!!?!

The doctors are titillated beyond words, and bump each other in a bizarre mockery of lesbian lovemaking.

HERMAN

Well, yeah, I guess so.

DR. RAZOR

Swell! That's been my favorite fantasy for years!

DR. WEENER

(honk)

HERMAN

Well, YOU'RE NOT MINE!

He tosses the doctors aside.

DR. WEENER

(honk)

Dr. Weener exits in a huff.

DR. RAZOR

I couldn't agree more, Dr. Weener. Why you—you're nothing more than a wolf in cheap women's clothing! I have my limits, my morals, and my ideals! You're obviously not a real woman. Still, you're awfully cute—can you get the money together?

HERMAN

How much?

DR. RAZOR

Let's see, the bait shop needs—I mean, I'll need nine thousand dollars, and I'll need it stat—whatever that means.

HERMAN

I don't have that much now.

DR. RAZOR

Then go, and never darken my office door again. You want an ori-fice? Don't come to my office *(pronounced to rhyme with "orifice")*! Not until you get the money! I mean, not until you're more of a woman! Good day, sir!

HERMAN

I'm a transsexual lesbian, I said.
Good-bye, they all said.
That's just too much to handle, they all said.
One or the other, maybe, they all said.
But both, they all said, good-bye.
Good-bye.
Good-bye.

ACT II, Scene 5

DOC GRINDER

Sound under: percussion music. Doc is now very femme and does the following as a macabre send-up of Laurie Anderson. Or maybe it's Rod Serling. One of those cultural icons.

Good-bye.
Hello.
It's now.
It's what you've been waiting for.
The woman destroys herself
to envision man.
The man destroys himself
to envision woman.
No simple masquerade, this.
To truly become the other gender,
the first gender must be
destroyed.

HERCULINE

My name will be Abel.
Child of peace, victim of aggression.
Beloved of God, slain by his brother.
Mourned through the ages.

DOC GRINDER

Sweet, and the boy?

HERMAN

My name will be Katherine. It was the name of a girl I
wanted to be all through grade school.

DOC GRINDER

How childish.

HERMAN

Child*like*.

DOC GRINDER

Very well, children,
then walk in the sun
and let the flame of the public eye
burn away the remnants of
the man
the woman
you have been all your life.

Doc stalks offstage. Rhythmic bells begin to play. Herculine and Herman are losing their gender identities, each becoming more androgynous in the following dance. The lines are said in an overlapping fashion, rhythmically in time with the music, and repeated at the discretion of the actors and choreographer.

HERCULINE / ABEL

They're looking at me.
Their eyes are burning me.

HERMAN / KATE

They're looking at me.
Their eyes are burning me.

HERCULINE / ABEL

Is it my body?

HERMAN / KATE

Is it my hair?

HERCULINE/ABEL

Is it my voice?

HERMAN/KATE

Is it my skin?

HERCULINE/ABEL

Is it my movement?

HERMAN/KATE

Is it my movement?

HERCULINE/ABEL

Is it my emotion?

HERMAN/KATE

Is it my ambition?

HERCULINE/ABEL

They are . . .

HERMAN/KATE

. . . looking at me. Their eyes . . .

HERCULINE/ABEL

. . . are burning me.

HERMAN/KATE

I'm to be a woman, I said to the man
I once had been, good-bye he said.
Oh god, I'm disappearing.

HERCULINE/ABEL

It is as though I come apart from

myself. No longer woman, not yet
a man. Standing outside.
Bidding myself adieu.

*They have no more identity. Herman becomes One. Herculine
becomes Another. They hear each other for the first time, and
search for one another.*

ONE

Good-bye?

ANOTHER

Good-bye?

ONE

Good-bye?

ANOTHER

Good-bye?

*They find each other onstage and embrace silently as part of
the dance. The music stops.*

DOC GRINDER

*Doc speaks from the rear of the audience, or over a speaker
system. It's his most human moment.*

Can anyone here remember the moment you fell asleep on
any given night? A few minutes before, maybe—or even a few
moments after. But the exact moment that divides asleep from
awake—never. My mother keeps trying to remember that

moment. She says that if she can remember that moment—if she can just capture that moment—she'll have a handle on death.

The music of bells begins again, as the two onstage dance with each other.

ONE

You're so beautiful.

ANOTHER

You. You're so beautiful.

ONE

You. While they're watching?

ANOTHER

Who?

ONE

Them—oh.

ANOTHER

Are you . . . are you mad?

ONE

I feel I am.

ANOTHER

While they're watching?

ONE

When I was young, I would hear voices in the thunder.

ANOTHER

I would see faces in the branches against my bedroom window.

ONE

You're so beautiful.

ANOTHER

You.

ONE

Is this acting?

ANOTHER

Is this dialogue?

ONE

Are we alive?

ANOTHER

Have we ever been more alive?
Are you breathing?

ONE

Can you feel me breathing?

ANOTHER

I was taught in school that God created all creatures male and female.

ONE

So, God was divisive from the start.

ANOTHER

And that Adam was jealous of the love the beasts and birds could express to one another.

ONE

So, rather than let Adam learn to love himself, this God stepped in, split Adam in two, and said here—love something outside yourself.

ANOTHER

That is not how I learned it, but yes. Yes.

ONE

I was taught in school that the greatest contribution to modern mathematics was the concept of zero. I never knew zero 'til now.

ANOTHER

Then zero must be the point where people and their ideas move out beyond their boundaries to become their opposites.

ONE

That is not how I learned it, but yes. Yes.

ANOTHER

Are we acting?

ONE

Is this dialogue?

ANOTHER

Do we have time?

ONE

While they're watching?

ANOTHER

Are you . . . are we mad?

ONE

Most likely.

ONE AND ANOTHER

Then breathe.

They embrace again, breathing together. Doc Grinder enters, once again male. Unnoticed, he tiptoes over to them and mimics their ballet-like movements.

DOC GRINDER

Well, what's up, said doc.
What's comin' down.
How's tricks?
What's . . .

He laughs, realizing what he must do.

What's in a name!

He snaps his fingers, the music stops, and the two break apart, each more clearly gender-identified and individuated. As they are named, each becomes solidly the other gender. Doc walks into the audience, sitting in an aisle to watch the rest of the scene.

KATE / HERMAN

What's your name?

ABEL

Abel.

                    KATE/HERMAN

You're a man?

                        ABEL

Does it matter?

                    KATE/HERMAN

It's beginning to.

                        ABEL

Your name is . . . ?

                        KATE

Kate.

                        ABEL

Then you're becoming a man?

                        KATE

I'm becoming a woman.

                        ABEL

Is this acting?

                        KATE

Seems like it.
Is this dialogue?

                        ABEL

Yes.

They exit separately.

DOC GRINDER

Walks back up to the stage. He is not untouched by their separation.

> Neither shall remember having danced with the other.
> Fragments—sketches—bits of this moment
> shall return to each
> in their dreams.
> But hey—hey, Perfesser!
> Gimmee that old postpartum rag!

He snaps his fingers. Piano version of Gershwin's **Rialto Ripples Rag**.

Act II, Scene 6

COOK

In the original production, the Cook was played by the Herman/Kate actor, à la Julia Child. She manipulates a large wad of bread dough, shaped like a penis, using a variety of surgical instruments. The words she speaks are verbatim from my surgeon's report.

Under general anesthesia after routine preoperative preparation and draping, the patient was placed in the lithotomy position. Penile inversion technique genital conversion surgery is accomplished. Incision was made over the scrotum in the midline. The scrotal skin and . . .

CLERK

In the original production, the Clerk was played by the actor playing Herculine/Abel. The words he speaks are verbatim translations of the actual civil record in the case of Herculine Barbin.

By the judgment of the civil court Saint-Jean d'Angely, dated 21 June 1860, it has been ordained that the birth record of Herculine Barbin should be rectified in this sense . . .

COOK

Then with finger dissection, we continued to form the large vaginal cavity. Once this was done, a large pack was placed in the area, and we returned to the penile skin, into which we placed a plastic tube, while the lower third of the penile skin was completely denuded. This was to act as a skin graft within the vaginal cavity. The posterior aspect of the orifice was accomplished primarily with chromic catgut sutures utilizing . . .

CLERK

Amendment one—that the first name Abel shall be substituted for the first name Herculine . . .

COOK

We then tailored a labia majora, excising out the excessive scrotal skin, and returned to the before-mentioned purse-string suture which was now pursed in such a fashion as to not obliterate the blood supply but as to purse the new clitoris in an outward direction. The patient withstood the procedure well and returned to the recovery ward in good condition.

She places a small birthday candle in the vagina-shaped dough and lights it.

CLERK

Amendment two—that the child registered here will be designated as being of the masculine sex. So the record shall stand in the case of Abel Barbin.

Blackout. The two characters exit in the dark.

ACT II, Scene 7

A single spotlight comes up on Doc, still male, seated on his stool.

DOC GRINDER

We wouldn't leave you hanging there. Let's give these kids—what? Three years? Sure—time enough for them to discover that there is no acceptance for their kind—not one hundred years ago, and certainly not today. And so—three years have passed.

Believe it. Hey—trust me!

He exits as the lights go down. Deep-toned church bells sound.

ACT II, Scene 8

ABEL

Walks onto the stage, dressed in black with a white shawl. He is in a graveyard, speaking to the tombstones.

I was such a fool to have believed! To have trusted! To have obeyed! To have thought I would have enjoyed this. Who were you with such a grand stone? Cardinal Lefevre! How fitting that you lie there and I tread upon your bones. Tell me, Cardinal, tell me now that you are beyond it all—tell me what are the rules. Tell me how I, raised to be passed from father to husband, from one man to another—tell me how I am to be a man! How would you know—you got into skirts just as soon as you could.

Something I cannot recall about the significance of zero.

Oh, Grandfather, Poppy—you and your sister were the only two who let me be the preposterous woman that I was. It mattered not to you. Grandpappa—I am not a successful man. I spent my life in a world of women—the only men I knew were the priests and you, Poppy.

Excuse my deplorable manners—how is your new neighbor, who? Ah yes, Captain Bordeaux! Good evening, Captain. Tell me, Grandfather—is the distinguished captain scandalized by me? Most of Paris is.

The incessant struggle between nature and reason exhausts me more and more each day, and drags me with great strides toward the tomb. It is no longer years that remain to me but months, days, perhaps. I feel that in an obvious, terrible way, and how sweet, how consoling this thought is for my soul. Death is there. Oblivion, there. There without any doubt the poor wretch exiled from the world, shall at last find a homeland, brothers, friends. And there, too, shall the outlaw find a place.

Grandpappa—can you recall the moment of your death? I cannot even recall the moment I fall asleep, though I try and try. Is death like that moment? I believe my mother always wondered about that.

He kneels, placing the white scarf on the tombstone. He addresses either the audience or the other graves, or both.

Can any of you tell me the answer to that? Can any of you tell me how I can be a man when I am both man and woman? Can any of you light a candle for me?

Lights fade to black, and the church bells toll slowly as he walks offstage.

ACT II, Scene 9

*Cold lights come up to reveal Doc in top hat and tails, walking downstage toward the spot where Abel had just been. He begins to kneel but catches himself, watching the audience warily. He struggles with the decision, then kneels to the scarf, slowly picking it up, his face contorted with grief. He buries his face in the scarf. He slowly rises, pulling the scarf away from his face, revealing a hideous grin. Music in: disco version of **Ding Dong the Witch Is Dead** by Klaus Nomi. He laughs.*

DOC GRINDER

It's party time!

He moves into the audience, speaking to them over the music. He directs these lines to different audience members.

Hey—I told you to defend your gender—but you wouldn't listen, and now there's hell to pay!!! Now you—you look like you could use two bottles of blue, am I right? Of course I'm right! I've got a special for you—four bottles for the price of five—you'll love it!

And you—I've been looking at you all evening, and I still can't figure you out—what'll it be, pink or blue?

Kate enters, fully female now, and cuts music off abruptly with a sharp whistle.

DOC GRINDER

HEY! HEY, YOU CAN'T STOP THE SHOW LIKE THAT!

KATE

I just did.

DOC GRINDER

I'll have you written out of the show! I'll have you replaced! There's plenty of freaks like you in this town.

KATE

Go ahead—make my day.

DOC GRINDER

Not very womanly, are we?

KATE

Striking an overly "feminine" pose.

Maybe not.

DOC GRINDER

And certainly not much of a man.

KATE

Maybe I'm neither.

DOC GRINDER

Oh NO! You answered all these questions!

KATE

Maybe my answers bred new questions. New rules to break. New lines to cross.

She goes over to Doc's stool and sits down on it.

DOC GRINDER

Absolutely delighted that she is about to make a fool of herself.

And you want the stage? Go ahead! Make my day! Go ahead.

He strides into the audience, sitting down to watch what she does.

Act II, Scene 10

KATE

She picks up a candle from Herculine's nightstand and lights it.

Abel died an artful death. He shut all the windows in his flat and turned on the gas from every possible fixture. An artful death at his own hands. Death and gender were once the property of the individual. Soon they were taken over by the community, the church, the medical profession, the state. His was not a medicalized death. It was then *(blowing out candle)* art.

Something I don't remember about the significance of zero.

Doc Grinder laughs abruptly from the audience.

As to being a man or a woman, must I be one or the other? Must you? Do you know what one is, or the other?

DOC GRINDER

Moving rapidly back to reclaim the stage. Grandly.

A man has a penis!

KATE

I'm constructing myself to be fluidly gendered now.

DOC GRINDER

A woman has . . .

He searches for the right word. Kate waits, expectantly.

. . . no penis!

KATE

Do you know what you're constructing?

DOC GRINDER

Men have sex with women.

KATE

Because you and I are constructing our gender nearly every waking moment.

DOC GRINDER

Women have sex with men.

KATE

I need to be aware of constructing my gender, that's all.

DOC GRINDER

I can have all this enforced in any court in the land!

KATE

Oh really? Well, I used to have a cock, and now I don't. I have a cunt. And I still fuck women, and women still fuck me. If the right man came along, I might fuck him.

I don't consider myself a man, and quite frequently I doubt that I'm a woman. And you—you still think gender is the issue! Gender is not the issue. Gender is the battlefield. Or the playground. The issue is us versus them. Any us versus any them. One day we may not need that.

But, today? I live well, if underground. Nowadays, when I sit alone in my father's chair, sometimes I leave a quarter. Sometimes I don't.

I've said my piece, and I feel . . . curiously relieved. I feel fulfilled. You work out the rest, if you have the energy for it. The outlaw has found her place.

She turns and exits.

Act II, Scene 11

DOC GRINDER

He is stunned, turns to face the audience, and begins to applaud.

Bravo! Bravo! Bra—Brava!!! BRAVA! It gets very confusing, doesn't it?!? Wonderful words—just . . . wonderful words.

To the departed Kate.

Don't expect any federal funding for them though!

To the audience.

I know what you're thinking. You're thinking that he . . . she . . . oh let's just say she, shall we? You're thinking that . . . she . . . made . . . her point. Good point, too. Damned good point. In theory.

But that's got nothing to do with you and me.

I'll tell you something—we're going to go home tonight, you and I—and before we fall asleep we're going to say, thank heavens at least I'm a man. Thank heavens, at least I'm a woman. They can't say that!

Grinder's theme music back in. He laughs in triumph.

But you say you're a bit unsettled by all this? You say you need some help? I say I've got it for you—in the pink and blue bottles! You just come see me backstage. Thank you—so much—for coming this evening.

Curtain

Maggie, the goddess-in-training, in the first production of The Opposite Sex Is Neither, *directed by Iris Landsberg.*

the punchline

It was right around the time I started writing this book that my female lover, Catherine, became my boyfriend, David. It was right around that time that everything I'd been thinking about gender got thrown back into the blender. And that really made me think. That really made me throw up my hands and say, "Here we go again!"

The Opposite Sex Is Neither *at P.S. 122, New York City, 1993, directed by Iris Landsberg.*

16

THE SEVEN YEAR ITCH

(What Goes Around, Comes Around)

> This was written and delivered as a spoken-word piece for the grand opening of Red Dora's: The Bearded Lady Café in San Francisco in May of 1993, the seventh anniversary of my gender confirmation surgery. They asked me to speak about how to be a girl. After the two years I'd put into writing the text of the first edition of this book, it was very freeing for me to write something for the stage. Months after that reading, my editor, Bill Germano, contacted me saying he needed something to bring the book to a close. This is what I sent him. I still perform this piece onstage, and I'm happy that it's here for you to read.

I remember reading somewhere that it takes seven years for the human body to regenerate itself completely. That means in one seven-year period, every cell in our bodies dies and is replaced by a new cell. So the body you are wearing right now probably hasn't got one cell in common with the body you were wearing, say, seven years and six months ago.

As a species, we die and rebirth ourselves every seven years.

Now, this has some very interesting implications for a person like me. This past May, May 1, I reached the seventh anniversary of my genital conversion surgery. That's what they call it now when they wanna be polite. It's what we all mean when we say "the surgery."

As in, "When did you get the surgery?"
Or, "Are you going to have the surgery?"
Or, "How much did the surgery cost you?"
The surgery is where they laid my penis out on a table,
slit it up the middle,
and gutted it like a fish out of water,
then sewed it up
and poked it back up inside me,
kinda like turning a sock inside out.
And this is my vagina.
Same cells, different cell-block.
Man-made.
So seven years have gone by
since the surgery,
and all these cells I'm wearing
and all these cells I'm bearing
and all these cells I'm being
they're all brand-new.
Technically speaking, this body is homegrown.
Just like yours.
Ninety-nine-and-forty-four-one-hundredths percent pure.
Like the Ivory girl.
Maybe we belong to the same club after all.
You and me.

See,
I keep looking for that club
I keep looking for a home
I keep checking out the roll books

And I haven't found my family name anywhere.
I keep looking for the uniforms
I keep listening for the anthem
I wanna learn the right dance step
But my family's been carded at the door
And anyway,
If they let us dance,
Me and my people,
If they let us dance,
Who would lead?

Growing up, I would read these books. They all had passages like:

I couldn't wait for Aunt Peg and Lisa to leave the house. I immediately went into Lisa's room. My heart was pounding. I went to Lisa's dresser looking for her underwear. When I pulled open her lingerie drawer, I just stopped and stared in silence as I gently pulled out her panties, bra, slips, and other items one at a time and held each in front of my naked body. I slipped into a pair of panties along with a bra I'd stuffed with tissues. I then pulled on a beige half slip. Seeing myself in the mirror was so exciting and just as I was beginning to rub my silken encased penis, I was shocked by Lisa's voice saying, "Well, which of my dresses are you going to wear?"

—Anonymous, The Male Majorette, c. 1967

In the erotica of my people, we are always discovered.
Discover me.

In the '60s, when I was a hippie boy, I really believed the Beatles and Alan Watts and Kahlil Gibran and I guess even the Maharishi that love was all you needed.

My hair was longer then than it is now.
I wore beads and bell-bottoms.
I said things like *Far out* and *Groovy*.
All the people around me were in the peace movement.
But I never really understood the peace movement
because I never understood
peace.
I was too much at
war
with myself, I guess,
and I never got close enough to the war inside me
to compare it to the war that was going on all around me.

Like the guy who lives up the block from me now. We're at war, he and I.

He hangs out getting drunk with the street people in front of the video store across from the Safeway. He follows me home.

If I'm walking out my door and he's nearby, he'll say, "Mmmmm, just in time." I made the mistake of smiling at him the first day. He said, "Wanna suck on those tits, bitch."

Seven years and six months ago, these breasts weren't around to get me in trouble like that.

Now, he comes up to me if I stay in my car too long.
He licks his lips.
He rubs his hand over his crotch.
My mother never raised me to deal with this.
I haven't spent my lifetime learning how to deal with this.
Each time I see him, I feel like a deer on the highway, caught in the headlights of an oncoming truck.

Fifteen years after my hippie-boy stage

(or two complete bodies later, depending on how you're
gonna calculate time),

when I went through with my gender change,

when I had the surgery,

when they raised and lowered that knife,

when they cut through the blood and bone and nerve,

I thought to myself, Now I'm gonna know some peace of mind.

When they picked up a needle and thread

and sewed me back together again,

I said to myself, Now I'm gonna find my contentment.

And when I lay there healing and the pain was so intense

that all I could do was keep on crying,

I said to myself, The war is over,

let's build myself a memorial to the dead.

But it didn't work out that way.

There were still wars going on in my brain.

I wonder what makes these little cells so smart. I mean, you'd
think if they'd once formed a penis, they might recombine into
another penis after seven years. But nope. Nope. They do what
they last remember having been. These little cells remember to
re-form themselves into a vulva and vagina, such as mine are.

And what about those dead and dying cells . . . the ones that
disappear? No one talks about *them*. Where do *they* go?

> Somewhere, out there, there's a complete dead man's body, disassembled into micro-units—like those transporters do on **Star Trek**. Beam me up, Scotty. There's no life for me down here.

Somewhere, over the last seven years of my life, I left behind me
all the cells that add up to a body out there that looked remark-
ably like this one, like the one I built with the food I would eat and
the alcohol I would drink in order to avoid dealing with my life.

Look at me
All of me
My transsexual body is going on display
Wednesdays through Sundays
at Josie's Cabaret and Juice Joint
Come one, come all and
Look at me.
These breasts are real, y'know, I grew 'em myself.
This vagina cost more than the car I drive
But only if you don't include insurance
and I've got the no-fault kind
the cheap kind
I'm an assigned risk
Hey!
These stretch marks are real too
I got 'em by being the fat kid in grade school
See, I ate my way through all my questions
It was them or me, and my questions were eating me
day and night.
My questions stayed down deep
Right down there with my comfort
My questions were chewing on my heart while I chewed on
my Hostess Twinkies
my M&M's
my red licorice
and Grandma's chicken fricassee
I chewed it all and I never tasted a bite.
All I could taste was my burning heart.

I never stopped reading those porn books.
I still have a small collection of them.

*"Oh my God," said Faye as she buried
her face in her hands. "What are we going to do now?"*

"I have a little plan for our friend Frank here," Helen laughed. It was an unpleasant laugh. "He's been snooping around and asking so many questions that he's really gotten on my nerves. After what he did to you down on the beach, Faye, I can bring charges of immoral conduct against him, and . . ." She paused, then continued menacingly, "I have a picture to prove it."

"What do you want me to do?" I said, sitting down on the boudoir chair.

"Well," she replied, her voice as cold as the steel of the Magnum she held. "Well, since you are so interested in women, I think you should be given an opportunity to learn more about them—more completely—from the inside out, you might say. You'll have to learn to respect women and the best way to learn is through direct experience. Mr. Frank Martin, you will take the place of Mildred, the maid, for the next three days. If you satisfy us, we will tear up the photo and never say a word about what you tried to do to Faye."

She must be kidding, I thought. Me, as a girl? Ridiculous! But then I looked down the barrel of the gun she was leveling directly at me. "I'll . . . I'll d-do anything you say," I said, frightened.

"Oh goodie," giggled Faye, waving her gun. She was overjoyed.

—Anonymous, The Case of
the Accidental Murder!, c. 1962

In the erotica of my people, we're nearly always forced into our
change.

I guess I was forced into it.
I guess you might call the pornography a force.
I guess you might call all the advertising a force.
You might call the doctors who kept telling me
that if I wasn't a man, I had to be a woman,
you might call them a force.
You might call the fashion industry a force.
On the other hand,
you might call forcing someone to be one gender or another,
you might call that
a fashion.

> I am not a man.
> I am not a woman.
> I like playing.
> I've always loved make-believe!
> Of all the options I've got, I like being a
> girl the best.

I grew this body.
It's a girl body.
All of it.
Over the past seven years every one of these cells became
girl,
so it's mine now.
It doesn't make me female.
It doesn't make me a woman.
And I'm sure not a man.
What does that make me?

"Wanna suck those tits, bitch."

I'm supposed to be writing about how to be a girl. I don't know how to be a girl. And I sure don't know how to be a boy. And after thirty-seven years of trying to be male and over eight years of trying to be female, I've come to the conclusion that neither is really worth all the trouble. And that made me think. A lot of people think it *is* worth the trouble. And that made me think. Why? Why do people think it's worth all that trouble to be a man? Why do people think it's worth all that trouble to be a woman? And hey, I'm not just talking about transsexuals here. I'm talking about men and women, maybe like you. I am so intensely curious about what it must feel like to be convinced you're a man. I'm sitting here tapping this out on my computer, and I'm thinking about who might be reading this; and I know that some of you really believe you are women. I want to get down on my knees in front of you, I want to get down on my knees, and I want to look up into your eyes and I want to say tell me! Tell me what it's like!

> The tall red-haired actress drops to her knees downstage center. She looks up at the audience, her face framed in an amber spotlight. "Tell me what it's like to know you're a woman," she says, her voice barely raised above a whisper. "Tell me what it's like to know you're a man. Tell me, please, because I never went to bed one night of my life knowing I was a man. I never went to bed one night of my life knowing I was a woman."

My favorite book in our house when I was growing up was the dictionary. We had this huge dictionary. It was the size of a million phone books. It had its own pedestal in the hallway of our house. And it had its own light on the wall, aimed right down on the tan leather cover and the gold leaf–edged pages. And when you turned on the light, it would shine down on that dictionary, and after a little while under the direct light, the leather binding would get warm and give off an intoxicating scent that I would inhale every time I came to look up a word, whenever I needed to know what something meant. I've come to associate the meaning of all the important things in my life with the smell of warm leather.

When I was little, and I would say to my parents, what does this word mean, they would say, "Go look it up in the dictionary, Albert." And I would run, I would run flying to that corner of the hallway, to get my daily shot of leather and truth.

I think I always knew there was sex in that book. But I had far too much respect for its aging and brittle pages to come right out and say, Excuse me, could you please tell me what I'm supposed to do with this thing hanging down between my legs? I mean, what would I do if it told me I was supposed to keep that thing? No, it was better not to look at all, I thought. So I never looked up sex. I let her sleep in the dictionary somewhere between *self-analysis* and *shady*.

I looked in other pages for Sex.

The dictionary was the first taste I ever got of the Information Age. It had information I needed. It had information I wanted. That dictionary had information I craved. I believed with all my heart that the dictionary in our hallway would tell me who I was, what I was, if only I could read it right.

And that's how I discovered the Information Age.
See, I wanted to be informed.

I wanted to be in the know.
I wanted the hall light on and somebody home.
I wanted to be clued in.
I wanted to be in the loop.
I wanted to wear a knowing smile.
I wanted to wear that smile like a beacon.
I wanted people to look at my smile and say,
There goes a girl who knows what she wants
There goes a girl who knows her way around
I wanted people to look at me and say,
There goes an Information Age girl.
But I was too busy for the Information Age
When I was a boy.
I was too busy eating, drinking, fucking, smoking, spending,
gambling my way away from the information I needed.

And so I gave that shit up. I just put it aside.
I just said no.
One day at a time.
Easy does it.
First things first.
Honk if you're a friend of Bill W.
I shed my addictions like a snake sheds its skin.
I shed my addictions 'til I got down to
who I thought I really was
shivering naked it was just me left
me and who I thought I was.
And one by one I shed who I thought I was too,
all the who's I thought I really was.
I am shedding my identities
like I shed my dead and dying cells.
And every time I open the dictionary,
and find my picture next to one of those words,
I tear the page out of the dictionary and I
swallow it whole

and I shit it out
that's what I do when they try to label me now.
I am tearing pages out of the dictionary.
Imagine my surprise when the next page I hadda tear out,
the page that was hanging around my neck,
the page I'd held close to my heart all this time,
so close it was choking me and I didn't know it
Imagine my surprise when I had to destroy
the page with the word *Lesbian* written on it.

> There's an old Jewish proverb: God created
> people because God loves good stories.
> Wanna real good one? Okay, here we go.

See,
My Girlfriend is becoming the man of my dreams.
She is becoming the man my mother always wanted me
   to be.
Catherine has become David.
Like the old button from the '60s:
"My Karma Ran Over My Dogma."
Can you imagine?
I wake up one morning,
A nice lesbian like me,
I wake up one morning,
and I'm living with a man!
There were some questions I didn't want to ask
and I've been having to ask them:
. . . could I live with a man as my lover?
and if I could do that,
. . . with a man as my lover, what was I?

I hadda stick around for this one.
I couldn't leave this guy.
I had to stand by my man.
Nuthin I can do,
Cuz I'm stuck like glue
to my guy!
Hey!
I can sing all those old love songs now,
Without changing the pronouns.

And, hey!
It keeps me moving.
See, it's been seven years since my surgery.
It's been seven years of crawling in the sun like a snake
while I shed my skin year after year after year
Trying to keep three feet ahead of the dictionary.
Trying to keep out of reach of the people who think
it's so important to be a man
Trying to keep out of reach of the people who think
it's so important to be a woman
I really don't understand those people
Do you?
I don't understand the people who want me to be a man
I don't understand the people who want me to be a woman.
Do you?
It's been seven years, and y'know what?
I still get a thrill
when I look at myself in the mirror and I see girl not boy.
It's a lark!
Girl?
It's a gas!
Girl?
It's a hoot!

Girl?

It's an identity I am working my way out of.

And by the time the next seven years have come and gone

My girl skin will be lying behind me in the desert.

Right next to my lesbian skin.

Right next to my man skin.

Right next to my boy skin.

By the time the next seven years have come and gone

I'll be the one the dictionary has trouble naming.

By the time the next seven years have come and gone

Nothing of this body is gonna be left for them to find.

Nothing of this body is gonna be around.

Get your last looks now, 'cause I'm changing already

And by the time the next seven years have come and gone

I'm gonna be new all over again.

ACKNOWLEDGMENTS

I want to thank the people who've helped me travel as far as I have.

With special love and gratitude to my mother, Mildred Bornstein, who has put up with an awful lot from me. From my mother, I learned how to be gracious under fire, how to look for the laughter in any situation, and, most importantly, how to say no, when no must be said.

You kept the love there through all the hard times. Thank you, Mom.

Thanks so much to Rose Pascarell at George Mason University, who first told me I should write this book, who nursed me through the fear and trepidations of it all, who read it in its shoddier stages, and with whom I was able to spend some of the more wonderful times of my life.

And to my friend Alice Zander, who taught me the principle that someone's life's work begins at the point where their great joy meets the world's great hunger. She also taught me what to do with my pocketbook at restaurants, and other neat femme-y stuff like that.

Thanks to Holly Hughes: your work inspired me to write at all, and I'm in awe of your talent and your courage.

With gratitude to the women of Split Britches—Lois Weaver,

Peggy Shaw, and Deb Margolin—who taught me that there can be so much heart in camp.

Thanks and love also to Daniel Mangin, my editor at *The Bay Area Reporter*, who brought me out as a writer; to Noreen Barnes, who helped me birth *Hidden: A Gender* in writing and onstage; and to Amy Scholder, who kept encouraging me to write in my own style.

To Sandy Stone, Caroline Cossey, Leslie Feinberg, Renée Richards, Rikki Ann Wilchins, Virginia Prince, Jan Morris, and Canary Conn, my deepest appreciation for blazing a trail through the virtual forest of gender.

Jim Barnhill and Don Wilmeth, for teaching me my theater skills at Brown University. Your continued faith has been a blessing.

To Suzanne Badoux, who showed me that politics could have a sense of humor.

To Rhonda Blair, who first lured me to an academic conference to present a paper on Gender and Performance.

Thanks to the following theater artists, producers, and production people who've made it possible to produce *Hidden: A Gender*, and/or helped me with the time to write this book: Karen Rosenfeld, Rebecca Kaplan, John Killacky, Eleanor Savage, Thomas Mulready, Lisa Rofel, Tim Jones, Sky Gilbert, Gwen Bartleman, Mark Russell, Susan Finque, Rick Rankin, Michael Kearns, Tim Miller, Jordan Peimer, Wendy Chapkis, Gabrielle, Bruce Lee, Del Rey, Howie Baggadonutz, Jane Hill, Ron Ehmke, Donald Montwill, Vicki Wolf, Chris Rushton, Stephanie Weisman, Laura Brun, Marian Shoup, Margie Ekeberg, Will Wilkins, and Catherine Blinder.

Thanks be to whoever handed down the Macintosh computer to Apple, and the tablets of word processing to Microsoft. Special thanks to Steve Zagerman and Carol Oppenheimer of Bananafish Software for the great program ThoughtPattern, in which I made and kept all my notes for this book. And to Mona Helfgott and Chuck Nadell at Inspiration Software for their indispensable program Inspiration, which I used to rough out and outline the book.

My appreciation to the Women in Theatre Program of the Association for Theatre in Higher Education Conference, for showing me there could be a balance between theory and practice of theater.

Bless also my friends Linda Donald, Nicole Grimmer, Ingrid Wilhite, Stewart Wilson, Lisa Farmer, Iris Landsberg, KayLynn Raschke, Caitlin Sullivan, Cynthia Bologna, Lourdes Tallet, Flo Camponile, Loren Cameron and Isabella Radsna, and Lynn Ablondi, for putting up with frantic calls at all hours, and for my neglect of their company for long months.

Thanks to my fellow Starfleet officers, especially the valiant crew of the U.S.S. *Republic,* for covering for me on missions I missed while preparing this book.

Thanks to Chris Kovick, who booked me for a reading at Red Dora's, the text of which became the last chapter of this book.

To the original production company of *Hidden: A Gender*: Noreen Barnes, Sherry Anderson, Lori Dovi, Bobby Tyler, Rick Garlinghouse, Jill Posener, Drew Todd. A special thanks to Ken Dixon and Doug Holsclaw at Theatre Rhinoceros, who commissioned *Gender* and supported its production.

To the incredible Lori E. Seid, who was the moving force behind getting *Hidden: A Gender* out of San Francisco and onto a North American tour.

To Dona Ann McAdams, my favorite photographer—your work moves me so deeply, and I am honored to have sat for you.

To Justin Bond: thank you so much for bringing Herculine to life, and for teaching me so much about men. To Sydney Erskine, thank you for your portrayal of Herman, and for your thoughtful counsel. And thanks to Cayenne Woods for your strength in keeping the show on the road on tour.

Love and gratitude for all the support and patience; for the time and the space; and most of all for all the magic to David Harrison, who when we first met and fell in love was Catherine Harrison, but who became David as I was writing this book, and so I've had to make room for the next book!

Thanks to Gwydyn for all the purring.

Special Note of Thanks for the Second Edition

Over the past twenty-five years, thousands of people all around the world have contributed to the more and more nuanced discussion of gender: teachers, students, authors, actors, activists, filmmakers, playwrights, performance artists, drag performers, bloggers, poets, religious leaders, conference attendees, and so on. It took all of our agreements and disagreements to bring the conversation as far as it has come, necessitating an update to this book.

Thank you to my literary agent, Malaga Baldi, for shepherding my writing over the past quarter century. Thank you to all the editors, copy editors, designers, production staff, and marketing staff who helped me hone my words. Thank you to all my readers and audiences for the encouragement and invaluable feedback.

Thank you to my dear partner, Barbara Carrellas, who, along with dozens of doctors and nutritionists, hundreds of nurses, physician's assistants, and hospital staff, and thousands of friends, has helped me stay alive through two years of cancer treatments. It worked! At this writing, I'm two and a half years cancer-free.

BIBLIOGRAPHY

Amadiume, Ifi. *Male Daughters, Female Husbands.* Avon, UK: The Bath Press, 1987.

Anonymous. *The Case of the Accidental Murder!* Tulare, CA: Chevalier Publications, c. 1962.

Anonymous. *The Male Majorette.* Vol. 11. Crossdressers Fiction Series. Thompson, PA: Echo Productions, c. 1967.

Barnes, Noreen C. A panel at the first International Lesbian and Gay Theater Conference and Festival, 1989.

Bolin, Anne. *In Search of Eve: Transsexual Rites of Passage.* New York: Bergin & Garvey, 1988.

Braindrop, Lily. "Kate Bornstein: Gender Bender/Mind Bender." *Taste of Latex,* Summer 1990.

Califia, Patrick. *Sapphistry: The Book of Lesbian Sexuality.* Tallahassee, FL: The Naiad Press, Inc., 1983.

Cameron, Loren. Personal conversation, 1993.

Chapkis, Wendy. *Beauty Secrets: Women and the Politics of Appearance.* Boston: South End Press, 1986.

Cossey, Caroline. *My Story.* Winchester: Faber and Faber, Inc., 1992.

Davis, Murray S. *Smut: Erotic Reality/Obscene Ideology.* Chicago: University of Chicago Press, 1983.

Deikman, Arthur J. *The Wrong Way Home: Uncovering Patterns of Cult Behavior in American Society.* Boston: Beacon Press, 1990.

Dibbell, Dominique. Personal conversation, 1993.

Dolan, Jill. "In Defense of the Discourse: Materialist Feminism, Postmodernism, Postconstructuralism and Theory." *The Drama Review* 33, no. 3 (Autumn 1989): 58–71.

Douglas, Ann. *The Feminization of American Culture.* New York: Avon, 1977.

Ehrenreich, Barbara. *The Hearts of Men: American Dreams and the Flight from Commitment.* Garden City, NJ: Anchor Press/Doubleday, 1984.

Emigh, John. "Hajari Bhand of Rajasthan: A Joker in the Deck." *The Drama Review* 30, no. 1 (Spring 1986): 101–30.

Feinberg, Leslie. *Transgender Liberation: A Movement Whose Time Has Come.* New York: World View Forum, 1992.

Finque, Susan. A panel at the first International Lesbian and Gay Theater Conference and Festival, 1989.

Frazin, Jim. "Kate Bornstein: On Gender & Belonging." *Anything That Moves*, Summer 1991.

Fussell, Paul. *Class*. New York: Ballantine Books, 1984.

Gaiman, Neil. *The Invisible Labyrinth*. Vol. 1. *The Books of Magic*, ed. Bob Kahan. New York: DC Comics, 1993.

Garber, Marjorie. *Vested Interests: Cross-Dressing and Cultural Anxiety*. New York: Routledge, 1992.

Garfinkel, Harold. *Studies in Ethnomethodology*. Englewood Cliffs, NJ: Prentice-Hall, 1967.

Halberstam, Judith. "Queer Creatures." *On Our Backs*, Nov/Dec 1992.

Harrison, David. Personal correspondence, 1993.

Hughes, Holly. Quoted from the film *Sphinxes Without Secrets*, 1990.

———. "Clit Notes." Josie's Cabaret and Juice Joint, San Francisco: 1993.

Kalweit, Holger. *Shamans, Healers, and Medicine Men*. Translated by Michael H. Kohn. Boston and London: Shambhala Publications, Inc., 1992.

Kessler, Suzanne J., and Wendy McKenna. *Gender: An Ethnomethodological Approach*. Chicago: University of Chicago Press, 1978.

Lao-Tzu. *Tao Te Ching*. Translated by Stephen Mitchell. New York: Harper & Row, 1988.

Leslie, Jacques. "The Cursor Cowboy." *Wired*, May/June 1993.

Liette, Pierre. "Memoir of Pierre Liette on the Illinois Country." In *The Western Country in the Seventeenth Century*, ed. Milo Quaife. New York: Citadel, 1962.

Lucas, Craig. "Keynote Address." The first International Lesbian and Gay Theater Conference and Festival, 1989.

Marc, David. "Comic Visions: Television Comedy and American Culture." In *Media and Popular Culture*, ed. David Thorburn. Boston: Unwin Hyman, Inc., 1989.

Margolin, Deborah. Personal conversation, 1989.

McCarthy, Susan. "Techno Soaps and Virtual Theatre." *Wired*, May/June 1993.

McDevitt, Faith. A panel at the first International Lesbian and Gay Theater Conference and Festival, 1989.

Miller, Tim. A panel at the first International Lesbian and Gay Theater Conference and Festival, 1989.

Millot, Catherine. *Horsexe/Essays on Transsexuality*. Translated by Kenneth Hylton. Brooklyn, NY: Autonomedia, 1990.

Munk, Erika. "Representation and Its Discontents." *The Village Voice*, September 6, 1988.

Nanda, Serena. *Neither Man Nor Woman: The Hijras of India*. The Wadsworth Modern Anthropology Library, ed. Peggy Adams. Belmont, CA: Wadsworth Publishing Company, 1990.

Newton, Esther. *Mother Camp: Female Impersonators in America*. Chicago and London: University of Chicago Press, 1979.

Nisker, Scoop. *Crazy Wisdom*. Berkeley: Ten Speed Press, 1990.

O'Flaherty, Wendy. *Women, Androgynes, and Other Mythical Beasts*. Chicago: University of Chicago Press, 1980.

Raymond, Janice G. *The Transsexual Empire*. Boston: Beacon Press, 1979.

Saffian, Sarah. "Kate: A Gender." *Issues Monthly*, February 1991.

SAMOIS. "Handkerchief Codes: Interlude I." In *Coming to Power: Writings and Graphics on Lesbian S/M*, ed. SAMOIS. Boston: Alyson Publications, Inc., 1981.

Seid, Lori E. A panel at the first International Lesbian and Gay Theater Conference and Festival, 1989.

Shaw, Peggy. Personal conversation, 1989.

Starhawk. *Dreaming the Dark: Magic, Sex, and Politics*. Boston: Beacon Press, 1982.

Starr, Kevin. "Indulging the Sisters." *San Francisco Examiner*, October 12, 1981.

Stone, Sandy. "The Empire Strikes Back: A Posttranssexual Manifesto." In *Body Guards*, eds. Julia Epstein and Kristina Straub. New York: Routledge, 1992.

Sullivan, Caitlin. Personal correspondence, 1993.

Vaughan, Diane. *Uncoupling: How Relationships Come Apart*. New York: Vintage Books, 1987.

Vidal, Gore. *Myra Breckinridge*. Boston: Bantam, 1968.

———. *Myron*. New York: Ballantine Books, 1974.

Weaver, Lois. Personal conversation, 1989.

Williams, Walter L. *The Spirit and the Flesh*. Boston: Beacon Press, 1986.

Yoshimoto, Banana. *Kitchen*. Translated by Megan Backus. New York: Grove Press, 1993.